Learn How to Study

Learn how to study

A Programmed Introduction
to Better Study Techniques

SECOND EDITION

Derek Rowntree

B Sc (Econ) Cert Ed
Senior Lecturer, Institute of Educational
Technology
The Open University
(formerly Senior Lecturer in Programmed
Learning, Brighton College of Education)

Macdonald and Jane's · London

For Mark and Leo
should they ever need it

© Derek Rowntree 1970 and 1976

First published 1970
Second impression 1972
Third impression 1973
Second edition 1976

Macdonald and Jane's Publishers Ltd
Paulton House
8 Shepherdess Walk
London, N1 7LW

Made and Printed in Great Britain by
Hazell Watson & Viney Ltd
Aylesbury, Bucks

ISBN 0 354 04009 X

Contents

iv

Preface

This book is written for students of *all* kinds. It will
certainly help you if you are a student in a college or
university, but it will also be useful to 6th-form students
and to those following courses by correspondence at
home. Whether you are nearing the end of your course
or are just beginning, whether you are confident or
anxious, successful or prone to failure, a little time spent
thinking about the job of study will be amply repaid.

The ability to study is not something we are born with
(like the ability to breathe)—it is a set of skills that must
be learned. Yet few of us have ever considered learning
to study: even fewer have been *taught*. But now, year by
year, an expanding army of students calls out more and
more loudly for some kind of *guidance* on how to set
about the job of studying effectively. Some colleges and
universities are arranging courses on how to study.
Several books have been written about study techniques.
This 'programmed' book is an attempt to introduce you
to some basic study techniques rather more quickly than
could be done in a college course and rather more
effectively than can be done in normal textbook style.

I hope, in the pages that follow, to persuade you to
think critically about an approach to study that has been
tested and found effective by large numbers of successful
students. Apart from gaining a basic language in which
to discuss study problems with your tutors and fellow-
students, you should also be enabled to evaluate

the various techniques we discuss and adapt them, where appropriate, to your own needs.

These techniques will include the planning and use of study time, making the best use of a textbook, improving reading and note-making ability, writing essays, learning from discussion, and dealing with examinations. Most of the book is 'programmed'—a kind of writing that calls continuously for active participation by the reader. Three of the chapters are in 'normal' prose, however, and to these you are expected to apply what you have learned in the rest of the book.

How to Use this Book

1   As I have said, most of the pages that follow are 'programmed'. That is, they are divided (by lines across the page) into 'frames'. Each *frame* is a unit of teaching, and each one calls for you to do something, or answer a question. Then the correct answer will be given to you at the start of the next frame—below the line.

For instance, you may be asked to think of the word (or words) that completes the sense of a sentence in which I have left a blank (or blanks):

And the correct answer (in *italics*) will be found at the beginning of the next —— below.

---

frame (This is the correct answer for frame 1.)

2   At other times, I will ask you to choose which of *two or more* words best fills the blank in a sentence. For instance:

The correct answer to this kind of question will still appear at the (*top/middle/bottom?*) of the next frame.

---

3 Yet again, I will sometimes ask you a *direct* question, and
you should decide your answer before going on to the
next frame to check. For instance:

Where do you expect to find the answer to *this* question?

At the top of this frame! (Of course, my answer may
often be worded differently from yours, and you will have
to decide whether or not you are correct.)

4 Sometimes I will ask you a question like the one at the
end of this frame—a multiple-choice question with two
or more alternative answers. With this kind of question
I will either simply give you the correct answer at the
top of the next frame as usual *or* I will give each answer
a letter (as below) and, according to your choice of
answer, you will go on to read one or other of the
lettered paragraphs in the following frame.

Why do you think a programmed book keeps asking
you questions?
  To try and trip you up. **A**
  To help you learn.   **B**
  To give you a test.   **C**
(Look in frame 5 on the next page for the lettered
paragraph corresponding to *your* answer.)

5 Why are you reading this paragraph? It is not lettered A, B or C, so it does not correspond with any of the answers. If you want to get the best out of a programme (or any other reading for that matter) you must watch out for clues that will help you *skip* material you do not need. Otherwise you will waste a lot of your time. Please go back to frame 4 and decide which of the lettered paragraphs you should be reading.

A. *I am glad to say you are mistaken. I certainly shall not be trying to trip you up. All my questions will be perfectly fair. If you think about the information you are given you should be able to answer them correctly nearly every time. But the questions do have a very important purpose. Please go back to frame 5 and work out what it is.*

B. *This is indeed the purpose. If you read to answer questions, the questions will keep you active, aid your concentration, draw your attention to the most important ideas, and keep you informed as to how well you are understanding them. In short, the questions will help you learn. Please go on to frame 6.*

C. *Testing is not the real purpose. The questions only test in the sense that they help you keep a check on your own progress: nobody else need ever know what results you're getting. No, the questions in a programme have a much more crucial function. Please go back to frame 4 and decide what it is.*

6 As you will have noticed, if you have glanced at more than one paragraph of the previous frame, an *in*correct answer to this kind of question leads you to further discussion on the point, and you may then be asked to try again.

Since all these questions are intended to help you learn, it is important that you treat them properly:

NB. Always decide *your* answer *BEFORE* checking the correct answer shown in the following frame.

Please try to avoid the temptation to glance ahead, for if you do you will not learn so well. The best plan is to keep a *sheet of paper* in one hand as you read, and move it down the page uncovering just one new frame at a time. Do not uncover the next frame until you have made your response to the one before it.

Thus, if you were following my advice, you (*should/should not?*) be able to see the correct answer to this question right at this moment.

---

should not (You would have had the answer covered.)

7   So find yourself a sheet of paper or card, and use it to mask off the frame following any one you are working on.

A few more *hints* and suggestions for getting the best out of this book:

1. Read the chapters in the order I have numbered them.
2. Take a break between one chapter and the next.
3. Do not read more than two chapters in any one day.
4. I give the approximate time required for each chapter, and it is wise not to begin on a new chapter unless you have about that amount of time available.
5. If you do have to break off before the end of a chapter, check back through the earlier frames to refresh your memory before continuing from where you left off.
6. For maximum effect, discuss the programme's ideas with tutors and with colleagues wherever you have the opportunity.

(NOTE: Throughout the programme I have used the word 'tutor' to stand in for tutor, teacher, lecturer, instructor, etc. Similarly, I have used 'college' to stand for college, university, 6th-form, correspondence course, etc.)

1 Why learn to study?

(Study time: about 25 min)

The Problem

1.1 Why, you might well ask, should you be expected to spend time reading and thinking about study? After all, haven't you spent most of your life in studying? This may be so, but are you sure that the *kind* of study you've done so far will produce results now that you are in college?

For instance, here are some statements about study made among a group of students recently:

'I sit at my desk for hours on end, but very little really gets done.'
'I seem to spend too much time on some subjects, and not enough on others.'
'I find difficulty getting started; I keep putting it off.'
'It's so difficult to know what's worth learning.'
'In lectures I find I'm either making no notes at all, or else I'm writing down every word the lecturer utters.'
'I can't seem to settle at any subject for very long.'
'I don't have enough time to fit everything in.'

This is just a selection from many such statements. (Perhaps you could even add one or two of your own.)

How many of these students sound *confident* about their ability to study?

None of these students sounds very confident about studying.
(Nor are they so very unusual in this.)

Higher Standards

1.2 Why is it that so many students get through school
without too much bother, only to find themselves in
trouble at college? Partly it is because standards are so
much *higher*. The student who was one of the best in his
6th-form may find he is now below average, among
colleagues who are all as good as or better than he is.
So, quite bluntly, work which once would have earned
him grades of A— or B+ may now earn him only C—
or D+.

To get the same amount of success in college, you'll
need to do (*less/no more/more?*) studying than you did in
school.

───

more

1.3 So higher standards will involve you in more studying
than you did at school. However, it is not just the
amount but also the *kind* of studying that must change.
Now why is this?
At school, everything was organised for you. You no
doubt had:
1. a full timetable;
2. compulsory class lessons;
3. 'private study' periods;
4. specific homework set for you most evenings.
On top of all this, you knew perhaps that your
teachers would:
5. carefully watch your progress from day to day;
6. quickly spot and correct any back-sliding;
7. even offer well-intended spoon-feeding if there was any
danger of your failing an examination.

2

In short, you didn't have to worry too much about how to spend your study time, and you knew that your teachers would make sure you learned.

Would you say this is all true of *college* also?

No, things are surely not so organised for you in college.

You Are Responsible

1.4 You are now given much more *responsibility* for your learning. You spend far less time in class, and the college timetable is unlikely to suggest when you should be doing your private studying. You can use your out-of-class time productively for work and recreation, or you can fritter it away doing neither very satisfactorily. You are expected to timetable your own activities.

Your tutors may give you several weeks to complete a piece of written work, and probably no-one checks to see how you are doing until the day comes to hand it in. You will be given a wide range of new reading to do, probably without being told that certain texts must be read by certain dates. How thoroughly you apply yourself to these learning tasks is entirely up to you.

In short, whether or not you succeed in your studies depends chiefly on . . .
　　how well you can learn?　　　**A**
　　how well your tutors can teach?　**B**

1.5 **A.** *Your tutors can help create a stimulating environment in which learning can take place—but this is not the same as teaching you. You must develop your own study methods, set your own targets, and be your own guide. Your tutors will back you up, and may even inspire your efforts, but yours is the responsibility to learn. Go on to frame 1.6.*

B. *If you really believe this you'd better throw in the towel straight away, or else prepare to change your attitude pretty drastically. In higher education the emphasis is very properly on the learner learning rather than on the teacher teaching. Please read paragraph A above before going on.*

How Do You Study?

1.6 To help you be realistic about your present approach to study, here is a quick questionnaire. Consider each question carefully and answer it honestly by writing 'yes' or 'no'.

1. Do you make out a timetable for the studying you will do each day?
2. If so, do you usually keep to it?
3. Do you usually study in the same place every time?
4. Do you find difficulty getting down to work at the start of a study session?
5. Do you get your written work in on time?
6. Do you try to contribute to class discussions?
7. If you are having trouble with your work, do you usually discuss the problem with a tutor?
8. Do you ever try to analyse your work to see just where you may be weak?
9. Do you usually glance through a chapter, making a preliminary survey before you read it in detail?
10. Do you frequently skip tables and graphs when they occur in your reading?
11. When you come across a word in your reading that you do not know, do you usually look it up in the dictionary?
12. Do you agree that memorising is the most important factor in studying?
13. Do you write notes in skeleton form (that is an outline of key words and phrases rather than continuous prose)?

14. In lectures, do you usually take notes just as fast as you can write?
15. Do you keep all your notes for one topic together?
16. Do you consciously use ideas you learn in one course to help you in some other course?
17. When you have to memorise something, do you usually try to do it all in one sitting?
18. Do you find it difficult to express your ideas in writing?
19. If an examination or test is sprung on you unexpectedly, do you get a low mark?
20. Do you sit up late studying the night before an exam?

Write your answers before going on to the next frame

1.7 The questionnaire you have just completed is based on one tried out by large numbers of college students. Successful students more often than unsuccessful students tended to give the answers shown below:

1. *Yes*	5. *Yes*	9. *Yes*	13. *Yes*	17. *No*
2. *Yes*	6. *Yes*	10. *No*	14. *No*	18. *No*
3. *Yes*	7. *Yes*	11. *Yes*	15. *Yes*	19. *No*
4. *No*	8. *Yes*	12. *No*	16. *Yes*	20. *No*

If you look again at the questions, and at these answers you will perhaps get some idea of the kind of approach that leads to success. If these answers differ much from your own, you may see where you need to re-consider your study habits.

What Is Study?

But before we get down to discussing the problems of study and what can be done to minimise them, we'd better try to agree on just what study is. Maybe you've been at it so long you've never stopped to define it. Well, have a try now:

What is study?

Write down a definition before you go on to the next frame.

1.8 Unfortunately, I can't tell what *your* definition is. However, you can compare it with the definitions below. Which of these definitions of study would you *most* agree with?

Following a course of lectures and set work. A
Being taught all there is to know about a subject. B
The memorisation of difficult subject-matter. C
The systematic pursuit of understanding. D
Preparing to pass a tough examination. E
Devoting all one's thoughts and energies to learning. F
I can't agree with any of these definitions. G

1.9 **A.** *You have taken rather a passive line here. Following a course is often part of study, but* not a necessary part. *If you were determined enough to set your own study goals and work out how to achieve them, you would be following nobody, yet you'd still be studying. How so? Please return to frame 1.8 and consider the other definitions.*

B. *I thought we'd already decided that learning was now your responsibility? Forget about being taught: those days are over. Higher education is largely a do-it-yourself job. (Besides, nobody ever learned 'all there is to know' about a subject.) Please go back to frame 1.8 and look for a slightly more realistic definition.*

C. *This is more like the definition of 'cramming' than of 'study'. You are not a sponge, fit only to soak up facts and figures. You are a human being with the ability to think about and understand ideas. We can store all the information we need in books, on film, and in computers: the human role is not to store information but to use it, analytically and constructively.*

6

Your study methods should reflect this emphasis. Please go back to frame 1.8 and look for a better definition.

D. *This definition does seem to be the best of the bunch (though perhaps not as good as yours). It emphasises the importance of understanding (rather than merely remembering). It indicates the active role of the student—pursuing rather than merely being led along. It brings in the word 'systematic'— implying a considered evaluation of the means to reach a specified goal. Please go on to frame 1.10.*

E. *It is a good thing to have firm targets, but your study should be doing more for you than simply enabling you to pass a particular examination. Exam-centred 'study' can too easily lapse into cramming. It is not enough merely to swallow information that can later be thrown up in the examination room. Your studying should involve you in thinking about and understanding your subject, and exam success will be just one by-product of these activities. Please return to frame 1.8, and look for a better definition.*

F. *Well, at least you've emphasised thinking and the use of energy, but I have the feeling you are over-doing things. It would be a very obsessive, impoverishing kind of study if it left you no thought or energy for other human activities—entertainment and recreation, for example. Please return to frame 1.8 and consider some less total definition.*

G. *Well, I'd have thought we had a pretty fair range of opinion here. Perhaps there are two or more that you simply can't decide between. Perhaps your definition is so different that nobody else could have predicted it. I suggest you take the first opportunity to discuss your definition of study with your tutors or colleagues. You might also usefully skim through all the paragraphs above (comparing each one with the answer to which it relates), before you go on to frame 1.10.*

1.10 *Study* involves you in deciding goals and choosing methods, solving problems, setting up tests or experiments, collecting information, separating facts from opinions, comparing facts and weighing up opinions, and looking for proof and truth.

It demands that you analyse and criticise not only your own ideas but also those of other people, whether you hear them in lectures or discussion, or read them in books and articles.

You will have to make concise notes and summaries to help you remember and to clarify your thinking, and you will have to express yourself clearly and to the point in writing essays, reports, and theses.

In fact, you will be applying all your critical powers to the quick and effective handling of information as you make your way towards definite goals.

If, for the sake of argument, you accept the above definition of study, for *how long* would you expect to be studying?

Well, I asked your opinion. Mine is that 'studying', in the sense I have described, is something you'll be doing for the rest of your life. (Presumably you will always be collecting and evaluating new ideas, relating them to what you already know, and perhaps explaining them to other people.)

Study as a Job of Work

1.11 Study is partly an attitude of mind, but it is also a *job of work* which, like any other, has its own skills and work habits which have to be learned. Of course, it takes time and trouble to learn the most efficient ways of doing any job, and it might seem easier just to muddle along. But, once learned, good work habits save untold amounts of time (your time) in the future.

Quite frankly, study will always be hard work. But efficient study techniques will make the hard work . . .

harder?　　**A**
easier?　　**B**
disappear?　**C**
productive?　**D**

1.12 **A.** *Only in the sense that it is harder,* at first, *to learn the crawl or breast-stroke when all you're used to is the dog-paddle. But when you've learned the more efficient method you can get along a lot faster. Similarly with the techniques of study. Return to frame 1.11 and rethink your answer.*

B. *Perhaps to some extent you are right. Efficient study techniques will allow you to produce better results in a shorter time, and you may well feel under less strain than previously. However, I believe you will still feel you are working hard, but with the encouragement of knowing you are achieving results. Read paragraph D below.*

C. *Never in this life. Study demands critical thinking and this always involves hard work. However, hard work is not always fruitful—it may be misdirected and fail to produce results. The purpose of efficient methods, in study as in any other job, is to make sure that your hard work is not wasted. You may have to work just as hard, but you'll have the encouragement of knowing that you are getting results. Please return to frame 1.11 and choose a better answer.*

D. *Efficient techniques will make the hard work more productive. That is, for a given amount of work done, you'll get more accomplished. The quantity and quality of your results will improve. You will get more done in a given time. Instead of working hard yet still feeling the job is getting on top of you, you'll work hard and have the satisfaction of knowing you are achieving results. Please go on to frame 1.13.*

The Importance of Motivation

1.13 There is one snag we must face. Not all students are really prepared to put in the thought and practice needed to learn new habits. Some believe they can get by as they are. Such students are simply not *motivated* to learn.

Lack of motivation is obviously a deadly enemy of effective study. It results in apathy, boredom, and a general desire to put everything off till another day. Unmotivated students are devoid of drive and imagination, and the spirit of enquiry is usually dead in them. They only do (usually grudgingly) what they are *told* to do. They cannot concentrate. They have difficulty remembering what they have studied.

Do you know any students who fit this description? Do you have any idea *why* they lack motivation?

Almost certainly you'll know some students who use little energy or imagination in the job of studying. It is not always easy to say why, however.

1.14 One reason for a particular student's poor motivation may be the fact that he is no longer being urged along by his school teachers and just doesn't know how to cope now he must think and plan for himself.

Another reason might be *lack of purpose:* he perhaps has no goals or objectives to aim at. Before you go on to the next frame, stop a moment and honestly answer this question in your own mind:

Why did you come to college?

1.15 *There are many possible answers, and only you know what yours is.*
Here are some of the possibilities:
1. To please my parents/teachers/friends/relatives, etc.
2. Because I did well at school.

3. The social life attracted me.
4. Because I wanted to train as a teacher/plumber/ doctor/engineer, etc.
5. I couldn't think of anything else to do.
6. To get some further education.
7. To pursue my interest in my subject.

Clearly, these reasons for coming to college are not all equally likely to help a student take the job of studying seriously.
1. Which reason is *least* likely to aid a student's motivation?
2. Which is *most* likely to motivate him?

---

1. *Probably 5 closely followed by 3.*
2. *Almost certainly 4 or 7—with 6 as a (rather vague) runner-up.*

1.16 Whatever the merits of other possible reasons for being in college, the student who is pursuing a *vocational* aim (4) or a strong interest in his *subject* (7) is the one most likely to develop a professional attitude to the job of studying.

Certainly a *lack* of interest in his subject is often the cause of a student's *poor* motivation. What would you recommend a student to do if he was genuinely *un*interested in his *course as a whole?*

The student who has no interest in his course as a whole might well be advised to stop it at once and start looking for something in which he could find satisfaction.

1.17 What more commonly happens, however, is that just *some* aspects of a course are less interesting than others. This is something we must learn to live with. It is up to the student to *put interest into* the dull areas, or they will damage his performance in the course.

What would be the best way of handling these uninteresting parts of a course?
a. Forget about them, or
b. Put them off till later, or
c. Work at them.

---

c. *Work at them.*

1.18 Be *extra* active in the subject that makes least appeal to you. Try to find out why it is important. Talk it over with tutors and students who *are* interested: what makes it attractive to them? (Other people's enthusiasm can sometimes be infectious.)

Approach the subject from a variety of viewpoints. Don't restrict yourself to one tutor or one textbook: find out how different tutors tackle it; ransack the library for the books that will bring the subject home to you.

Above all, try to relate the uninteresting subject to something that you *do* find interesting. (In teaching, one one must do this for other people; in learning, one must do it for oneself.) Remember that learning is basically *association*, and the more interests and knowledge you have, the more things you will have to associate new ideas *with*.

Thus, the more you have already learned, the (*harder/ easier?*) it will be to learn new things.

---

easier

1.19 New ideas only seem 'difficult' or uninteresting when you have no pegs (background) to hang them on. Making these pegs (building up your background in a subject) may seem arduous at first, but the going will become easier and easier—and more enjoyable. There is nothing more motivating than seeing that you have already made progress.

So, we can't always rely on interest to act as the *stimulus:* in some cases we must expect it as the *fruit* of study. If a vital topic is not already interesting, it is up to you to make it so—by an effort of *will-power* and *determination.*

NB. Before you go on to the next frame, pause a moment to write a rough note of the *main points* you *remember* being made in this chapter.

Review Questions
These next six frames contain questions that will help you check your memory of the main points of this chapter. If you find any question too difficult, you can get help by looking back to the frames mentioned in brackets after the question.

1.20 What are the two main differences between school and college learning that may call for improvements in the way you study? (Frames 1–5)

You'll face higher standards and you'll need to take more responsibility for your own learning.

1.21 How would *you* define study? (Frames 6–10)

Whatever your definition, I hope it implies an active *role for the student, a* systematic *approach, and the importance of* understanding *(rather than memorising).*

1.22 When do you expect to give up 'studying' in the sense you've defined it? (Frames 10–11)

1.23 As a result of learning the techniques of study will you expect to . . .
a. study every subject in exactly the same way?
b. spend more time on studying?
c. get more achieved in a given time?
d. learn everything without effort? (Frames 11–12)

c. *get more achieved in a given time.*

1.24 Which *two* of the following students would be *best* motivated to learn effective study techniques?
1. A man with a good school record whose chief aim in coming to college is to captain both the football and the cricket team.
2. A girl who has always been keen on archaeology and who wants to do research after finishing her undergraduate course in the subject.
3. The export sales-manager being paid by his firm to learn French and German who knows that his career prospects depend on the grade he achieves.
4. The middle-aged man who feels he has missed-out in life but that all will be put right if he can get into college to do some kind of course.
(Frames 14–16)

2 and 3

1.25 What should a student do if he finds his course lacks interest? (Frames 17–19)

If only a few parts of his course are uninteresting, he should look for ways of putting interest into them: (talk to other tutors, read other books, relate it to what he is interested in, and so on). If nearly all the course is uninteresting, he should seriously consider giving it up.

1.26 Go on to Chapter 2 when you are ready.

2 How to organise your studying

(Study time: about 35 min)

Why Bother ?

2.1 If you are anything like the majority of students, you'll have suffered from one or more of the following study problems:

1. You feel you simply aren't getting enough done.
2. You do all your work in exhausting fits and starts.
3. You take a long time getting started on a study session.
4. You waste time flitting from one study task to another.

Now there is only one way to solve, or (better still) avoid these soul-destroying problems, and that way lies through *planning* and *organisation*. You must *plan*; how much time you need devote to study; which subjects you will study when; what you intend to achieve during each study session. You must *organise* things so that these goals can be reached.

With effective planning you may even get *more* work done in (*a smaller/the same/a greater?*) amount of time.

a smaller (You are *certain* to get more done in the same amount.)

How Much Study Time?

2.2 The first step in organising your time is to work out how much time you've got to organise. Obviously, there are $7 \times 24 = 168$ hours in a week, but they won't all be available for study.

Every day you will spend perhaps a *third* of your time asleep, and maybe another couple of hours in eating and other necessary chores. Most days also you will have to do some travelling and attend some lectures and classes (or go to work, if you are not a full-time student). Only you can do the arithmetic and work out how much time will remain for you out of *your* 168-hour week.

It is up to you to decide how this remaining time should be divided between —— and recreation.

study

2.3 Recreation and leisure activities (sport, dancing, conversation, clubs and societies, cinema and theatre visits, etc.) are vital to your continued well-being and you should never let them get squeezed out of your timetable. Fortunately, the more you plan your work, the more time you'll find free for relaxation. Each *week* allow yourself:
1. At least *one* regular day off (completely free).
2. Perhaps one morning, one afternoon, and one evening free (preferably from different days).

Even when you have added together eating, sleeping, travelling, classes, and regular times off, you'll find you still have a fair bit of time at your disposal. Take the case of Bill Smithers who has the following weekly time-loads:

sleep	56 hours
eating, etc.	21 ⎫ (Probably more
travel	12 ⎬ than *you* spend?)
classes	24 ⎭
regular recreation (2 working days)	20
TOTAL	133 hours

Out of the week's 168 hours, this student still theoretically has —— hours left that he *could* spend on study.

---

35 hours (And this student spends rather more than most on eating, travelling, and attending classes. If you work out your *own* times you'll probably find, unless you are a part-time student, that you have quite a bit *more* than 35 hours to spare.)

2.4 But let's face it, few students ever do spend 35 hours a week on private study—except perhaps in the final delirium of exam preparation.

So how much time should be spent on study? I suggest you begin by planning yourself a *weekly minimum of 40 hours work*—to include lectures, seminars, practicals, and all the other timetabled sessions that you are expected to attend, *and* your own private study.

Thus, our Bill Smithers with his 24 hours of classes should spend at least —— hours on private study.

---

16 hours (This gives him a weekly minimum total of *40* hours work.)

2.5 Notice that I have put the stress on *minimum*. You should, with practice, be able to work for considerably more than 40 hours a week. But it doesn't do to start off with an over-ambitious plan that you can't possibly keep to at first.

Far better to start with a modest time-target and learn good work-habits: then, once you've got into the routine of doing regular successful studying, you'll find you can add on the odd hour here and there without any agony whatsoever.

During which college terms are you most likely to need to do *well over* 40 hours work a week?

═══

Well, you'll probably need to pile on the effort in any term with an examination or practical field work in it; and by the last two terms of your course you may well want to clock up 50 hours or more per week.

Making a Timetable

2.6 Don't just say 'All right then, I'll do 40 hours a week', and simply hope for the best. To make sure of reaching your quota you'll need to work out a timetable.

First consider:

1. Exactly how many hours available for private study? 40 *minus* lecture hours = (Probably between 15 and 30 hours.)
2. How should these hours be *spaced out* over the week?
3. At what *times of day* should they be used?
4. How should they be divided among your *subjects*?
5. What is the *minimum length* of time for a useful study session?

Let's answer that last question first. What is the smallest usable study session? I suggest you take as your basic study unit the *length of a normal college period:* that way you'll be able to take best possible advantage of gaps between your classes.

So I am suggesting you plan your study sessions in blocks of at least —— minutes.

45 to 90 minutes perhaps?

2.7 Are you thinking 'But I can't get anything done in 45 minutes!'? That may be because you normally have to spend 10 of them deciding what to spend the rest on. Once you get into the habit of planning what you want to achieve *before* the time for study arrives, you'll soon find you can make productive use of quite short stretches of time.

So, you have perhaps 18 hours of study to do, and you are going to look in your timetable for gaps of 45 minutes or more. To meet your quota you'll have to allocate a number of these gaps to study. Thus you will arrange with yourself to do 45 minutes on Monday mornings, 2 hours on Monday evenings, 1½ hours on Tuesday afternoons, and so on.

However, we can take this further:

Which of these two possible plans would be most likely to help you make productive use of Monday morning's study time?
a. You decide to spend 45 minutes on private study, or
b. You decide to spend 45 minutes studying Maths.

b. *You decide to spend 45 minutes studying Maths.*

What to Study

2.8 Planning how to spend your study time is a sure way of helping yourself make productive use of it. Always allocate your study times to *particular subjects*—not just to 'study'.

Now how do you *share* your time among your various subjects? Clearly, some subjects will need more time because they are more important to your course, or because they demand a lot of reading or writing up.

Again, you may decide your priorities according to how easy you are finding the different aspects of your course. Try making a list of your subjects with the ones you find *most difficult at the top* and the ones you have least trouble with at the bottom. Assuming all your subjects are of equal importance, those at the (*top/bottom?*) of your list should have a larger share of your private study time.

---

top

2.9 Generally speaking, it is wise to spend more time on the most difficult subjects. Review your list every couple of weeks though, because, as you go through your course, the areas of difficulty will probably shift about from one subject to another.

When to Study

So you should be able to share out your study time among the subjects on your list. Now whereabouts in the week's timetable will you slot in your study sessions? A good general rule is to do at least some of your study for each subject *as close as possible to the class period* for that subject. (Same day if possible.)

But *before* or *after* the class period? This depends on the form that class period usually takes:

When would be the most useful time for a *study session* if the class period is to be . . .

1. a straightforward informational lecture? (Before or after?)
2. a seminar or discussion? (Before or after?)

1. *after* (the informational lecture).
2. *before* (the seminar-discussion).

2.10 A study session right *after a lecture* can be used to review your notes, check that you really understood what was said, and follow up any references given. A study session just *before a seminar/discussion* gives you the chance to read up the background that will help you make an effective contribution in class.

One other factor affecting your choice of days for a particular subject is your own *temperament*. It may be, for example, that you find Tuesdays are best for tackling something new or especially difficult, while on Fridays you are too tired to do anything but background reading.

What should you do about these differences of mood when planning your timetable of study?
a. Try to overcome them, or
b. Take them into account, or
c. Ignore them.

b. *Take them into account*. (Assign your toughest subjects to the days you normally feel at your best.)

2.11 The next question is:
Which part of the day will you devote to which subjects? Partly again this will depend on the difficulty of the subject, and on the sort of work it involves you in.

Your toughest subjects (with the emphasis perhaps on unravelling a complex technical argument, rather than on

soaking yourself in narrative-type background) are best
studied . . .
a. in the mornings? or
b. after lunch? or
c. last thing at night?

---

a. *in the morning*. (When you are probably at your
freshest?)

2.12 Partly, it must be admitted, the timing of a study session
within the day must also depend on temperament.
Many students are captivated by the glamour of midnight
oil, and get a particular kick out of working when
everyone else is asleep. But this glamour can seem a bit
over-rated when you stagger bleary-eyed into a 9 o'clock
lecture the following morning. There's a lot to be said for
training yourself to complete your work by midnight.

You should now be able to fill out your *timetable* to
cater for:
1. Regular classes etc. (already timetabled for you).
2. Study sessions, each of at least —— minutes and each
   devoted to a particular —— (and some of them
   placed —— to the class period).
3. A total work time (1 and 2 together) of at least ——
   hours per week.
4. At least one complete —— per week booked firmly
   for regular recreation.
5. Time that can be used for recreation or for additional
   —— when the need arises.

---

2. *45, subject, close*   3. *40*   4. *day*   5. *study*.

A Sample Timetable

2.13 As an illustration, let's look at the timetable (page 25)
drawn up by Joe Grice—a first-year student in a
college of education, training to be a teacher. Joe has

about 19 hours of classes per week so, to make up 40 hours of work, he has scheduled another 21 hours for his private study. He decides to spread this time among his eight subjects as follows:

Subject	Study Time	Comment
Geography	6½	Main subject. Maximum time allocation.
Education	5¾	Actually finds this course more demanding than main subject but is counting on getting extra time free for study within the day that is entirely timetabled for Education.
Drama	2¾	Joe's subsidiary subject. He starts off giving it a modest allocation of time, but thinks he may have to increase this later.
English PE Art Music Maths	1 1 1 1 2	With four of these courses (all on how to teach a subject in school) Joe feels he needs spend very little time to keep on top of things. But Maths has always been his weak spot and he resolves to give it a little extra time.

total: 21 hours

In case any of these estimates proves insufficient (and realising that a session set aside for study will sometimes have to be used for some other purpose) Joe has allowed 6 hours (Thursday evening and Friday afternoon) which he could use to 'catch up' on any outstanding work by extra study. Otherwise, he will use these times for extra recreation.

Would you think this is *more* or *less* study than most students of your acquaintance actually do?

2.14 Joe's timetable probably calls for *more* study than most students actually do. However, notice this:

1. Only once does he start before 9.30 in the morning.
2. He finishes work by 9.00 each evening.
3. He has leisurely breaks for meals during the day.
4. He is free all Sunday, most of Saturday, and on one afternoon and one evening during the week.

In short, he has more spare time than most professional or business people, and more indeed than he himself will have when once started on his own career!

	Monday	Tuesday	Wednesday	Thursday	Friday	Saturday	Sunday
9.0							
10.0	MATHS	*Education*	DRAMA	ENGLISH	GEOG	*F R E E*	
11.0	coffee	coffee	coffee	coffee	coffee		
12.0	MUSIC *Maths*	EDUCATION	DRAMA	*Education*	GEOG		*F R E E*
1.0							
2.0	lunch	lunch	lunch	lunch	lunch	lunch	
3.0	*Drama*	EDUCATION	*Geog*	P.E.	*FREE or 'CATCH UP'*	*Geog*	
4.0	tea	tea	tea	tea		tea	
5.0	ART	EDUCATION	GEOG	*English* *P.E.*		*Geog*	
6.0							
7.0	dinner	dinner	dinner	dinner	dinner	dinner	
8.0	*Art*	*Education*	*Drama*	*FREE or 'CATCH UP'*	*Geog*	*F R E E*	
9.0	*Music*	*Maths*	*FREE*		*Education*		

NB. Regular class periods are named in TYPE.
Private study sessions are *handwritten*.

Check where Joe has placed his private study sessions in relation to his class periods:
One of his two Geography classes (Wednesday and Friday) takes the form of a lecture, the other a discussion. Can you tell which might be which?

If Joe followed our suggestion from frame 2.10,
Wednesday's will be the discussion class, because he
timetabled a study session just before it; Friday's class,
with a study session that evening, is likely to be the lecture.

Using Your Timetable

2.15 So, at the very first opportunity (like sometime today)
plan out your own study timetable, taking care to label
every space. (If you need comment on it, have a word
with your tutor.)

Where would you think it best to *keep* your timetable
once you have completed it?
a. On the wall above your bed where you'll see it every
   morning, or
b. In a notebook which you carry about with you, or
c. Within sight from the place where you do your
   studying.

---

b. *In a notebook which you carry about with you.* (You must
be able to refer to it at any time.)

A Daily Job List

2.16 Every morning you will look at your study timetable to
check which subjects you have planned to study at which
times. Then take it further. Ask yourself *what particular
work* you are going to do in each subject. The more
precise you are, the surer you'll be of getting results from
your labours.

Make a list (preferably on paper) of all the *things to be
done* that day. For instance, Joe Grice might have made
out his list for one *Thursday* like this:

'Check references and plan essay on "streaming".
Listen to tapes of children's poetry and write notes for
a follow-up lesson.

Check physiology notes; revise where necessary.
Work through mapwork exercises to prepare for extra
seminar tomorrow.'

Refer to your list (as well as your timetable) at intervals
during the day.

If, at the end of the day, you find you have *not*
accomplished all the things on your list, what might you
decide to do about them?

*Well, it's your decision, and it would depend on how
urgent the things were. One solution might be to add them
on to your list for the following day.*

2.17 Anyway, the main point is that planning a study timetable
for a *week* at a time helps you to see what your goals
should be for each *day*.
   However, your first timetable is not fixed and
unalterable for all time. Give it a week's trial run and
then ask yourself how successful it has been. Did you
manage to keep to it? Did you study the intended
subjects at the intended times? Did you get everything
done?

If the answer to any of these questions is 'No', what
might you *do* about your basic timetable before starting
the next week?

*Surely you would alter your timetable in the light of any
difficulties you had experienced with it. (You might need
to re-arrange your study sessions, share out your study time
differently, or even put in more study time.)*

Revising Your Timetable

2.18 Remember that your original timetable is simply a useful
basis from which to work: you will need to take a

critical look at it quite frequently to see whether any temporary or permanent changes are needed. For instance you may need to:

1. Spend more time on a new project or special assignment, or
2. Alter your share-out of time among subjects because of changes in their relative difficulty, or
3. Make up for study-time which you lost, for one reason or another, in the previous week.

How often would you inspect your timetable with this intention of revising it if necessary?

At the beginning of every week *if you are wise.*

2.19 Think well ahead when you are checking your timetable for the coming week. If you know the subject of an essay to be handed-in six weeks from now, the time to start planning and reading for it is now. Similarly, if you have tests or exams coming up, don't leave revision till the last moment. Revision sessions are more useful when *spaced-out* rather than when all lumped together. Try to think of each week's work in relation to the whole term, the whole year, and the whole course.

What is your reaction to these suggestions about planning your study activities for the week ahead?

I don't believe it would work.	**A**
I think it might be worth trying.	**B**
I haven't got the right kind of personality.	**C**
I think it would take up too much time.	**D**

2.20 **A.** *The evidence proves otherwise. Students who plan their work always have the edge over those who merely drift from one study task to another. The planners have a stronger sense of purpose and priorities, and they get more done in the available time.*

You may object to planning on other grounds, but not on the grounds that it doesn't work. It does! Please return to frame 2.19 and re-think your answer.

B. *This seems to me to be the right attitude. Many thousands of students have learned to plan their work and they have almost always reported how their performances have improved. They have a stronger sense of purpose and priorities, and they get more done in the time available. In the early stages, of course, you may have some difficulty in forcing yourself to plan, but do stick at it; once you get the knack you'll wonder how you ever let yourself waste so much time in the past. Please go on to frame 2.21.*

C. *If you haven't, nobody has. Let's face it, planning is the way to get a job done as quickly as possible with the minimum amount of fuss. Don't tell me you really want to muddle along, not knowing what you are going to be doing from one moment to the next, and probably spending twice as long as you need on every study task?*

The fact is that many hundreds of students whose first reaction was the same as yours have been amazed to find how much their performance has improved once they've tried seriously to plan their work for a trial period. For all you know, it may even be your kind of personality that profits most. Please think about it, anyway, and read paragraph B above.

D. *Certainly you may have to spend a whole evening working out your first timetable. A good deal of thought needs to go into it. But, thereafter, a few minutes a week is probably all you need to keep it up to date. The point is, this amount of time will be repaid over and over again in the increased productivity brought about by having a timetable that reminds you exactly what you have planned to do with each unit of time. Please read paragraph B above before you continue.*

Organising Your Study Sessions

2.21 So, with a well-planned study timetable, you should be able to start each day with a list of *things to be done* in your study sessions.

But some students say 'Even when I know what I'm supposed to study, I still don't get very much done in the time'. Such a student's typical 'study' evening may well go something like this.

Finishes eating (and chatting) about 7.30 p.m. (Had intended to finish at 7.0). Sits down at desk but spends first 15 minutes jumping up and down to fetch papers and books, sharpen pencils, wind clock, etc. Begins to write. Finds fountain pen needs filling. Goes to borrow ink from friend in another room. Finds friend with group of students discussing a new pop group. Stays to state point of view. Some time before remembers is supposed to be studying. Reluctantly goes back to room. Works solidly for next 20 minutes. Remembers a new L.P. record he has bought. Thinks surely can play it as background music. Attention now shared between record-player and reading. Begins thinking about next weekend. Goes out to ring girl-friend. Returns to discover it is nearly 10 p.m. and still nothing much done. Next 40 minutes spent frantically (but hopelessly) trying to make up for lost time. Following day tells friends he 'spent the whole evening studying'. And he believes it himself, because he only remembers how exhausting it all was.

Does this ever happen to you?

Your answer must surely be 'Yes', because, to a greater or lesser extent, it has happened to all of us.

2.22 This frittering away of time is the biggest obstacle to effective study, and the only known cure lies in *planning* and *determination*. Plan exactly what results you want to achieve; be determined about achieving them.

What Are You Going to Study?

In making up your daily list of jobs to be done, be *as specific as possible* about what you plan to do in each study session. (See frame 2.16.) The more precise you are, the more incentive you have to get on with it. Think always in terms of what you want to get done rather than merely of how much time you are going to put in.

For instance, below you'll see three possible items a student might put on his list of jobs to be done. Which of them would give him the best incentive to make effective use of his time?

a. 'Spend one hour on *Statistics for the Social Sciences*', or
b. 'Spend one hour on Chapter 5 of *Statistics for the Social Sciences*', or
c. 'Read and make a summary of Chapter 5 of *Statistics for the Social Sciences*.'

---

c. '*Read and make a summary of Chapter 5 of* Statistics for the Social Sciences.' (The more specific your goal, the more likely you are to work with concentration and get the job done in the shortest reasonable time.)

Where to Study

2.23 Ideally, you should be able to study anywhere—in a quiet library or on a crowded bus. But let's be realistic. Most of us can't entirely shut off our minds to distractions. So you need to study in a place that is as free as possible from new things and new people that might steal away your attention.

Also, you need a place that is firmly associated in your mind with serious study. Thus you can slip into the right *frame of mind* the moment you sit down.

So, would you think you'd study best in . . .
a *different* place every day? **A**
the *same* place every day? **B**

2.24 **A.** *In one sense you might find it refreshing to go to a different place each day. But only because there would be so many new sights, sounds, smells, and sensations each day that they would quite take your mind off work! (This wouldn't really help you.) Besides, you'd be losing the chance to build up an association between a particular place and work; such an association can be a very useful psychological aid. Please read paragraph B below.*

B. *Familiar places (like your own study bedroom or a favourite corner of the library) are likely to hold fewer distractions than new places. And, by constant association of work with a particular place, you can build up the* habit *of getting down to work when you arrive at that place. Please go on to frame 2.25.*

2.25 As for conditions of study, make sure your study place is well-lit and properly ventilated, and neither too hot nor too cold. (Admittedly, it can be difficult to get everything to your liking if you are living in someone else's house.) The *less* you are aware of your surroundings while studying, the better.

But do remember study is a job of work. Which of these students is most likely to do the job effectively?

(a)   (b)   (c)

b. *(at a table)*

2.26 The best position for study is to sit upright at a table or desk. Bed may be attractive but, once you lie down, sleep is likely to ensue. Even an easy chair may prevent you from doing real study.

So, try to stick to a regular study place. Get plenty of light, don't let the air get stuffy, or too warm or cold, and don't make yourself too comfortable. *Stay alert.*

Having decided your goal for the study session and sat down in your study place, what should you do next?
a. Wait for the urge to work, or
b. Start work straight away, or
c. Go through some sort of warm-up procedure.

b. *Start work straight away.*

Getting Started

2.27 Effective study is largely a matter of good work habits, and starting work straight away is one of the very best. Don't wait till you are in the mood, or you may have to wait forever. Don't think that you have to 'warm up' in some very individual fashion. Warm up and get into the mood by starting to work. Don't just sit, *do* something.

For example, you might begin by reviewing your lecture notes on the topic you are dealing with. Or you might try to write down the main points you remember from the last piece of work you did on the subject. In fact, it is usually a good opening gambit to spend the *first 5 minutes* of any study session *reviewing* what you last did on that subject. And preferably *write* something down.

Having got yourself started by —— ing what you did last time, the problem then becomes one of how to —— *(What would be your problem?)*

review

concentrate (How to do this will be most people's problem.)

Concentration

2.28 You can train yourself to concentrate and keep paying attention, but it takes will-power and persistence. These hints may help you:

1. If you find it difficult to concentrate on a particular subject, start off by studying it in *very short bursts* only. Don't give up a whole evening only to accomplish nothing. Put all you've got into 45 minutes at a time. If even this is a terrible prospect, cut it right down to, say, 20 minutes, but have something very *definite* to do. You must prove to yourself that you can keep hard at it, even if only for a very short spell. Gradually, you'll be able to build up to a basic *minimum* of 45 minutes.

2. If you find yourself day-dreaming, or drifting away from your goal; *stop it* immediately. Unless you are clearly in need of a definite break, force your attention back to the job you are trying to get done

3. In every hour of study you will perhaps need a *break* of between 5 and 10 minutes (or two shorter breaks). Stand up, walk around, turn your mind to something else. But take a clear break and then get right back to the job in hand.

So, if you find it difficult to concentrate, practice over very —— periods of study time, —— day-dreaming the moment it starts, and reckon to take breaks totalling up to —— minutes in every study hour.

2.29 Another aid to concentration is to *make notes*. Do try to make some sort of record of what you have achieved in the time you've spent on study. Apart from keeping you active and alert, these records will help you review later.

Ending a Session

Try not to finish a study session at a tough spot in the subject. This will make you less than eager to return to it next time. Aim to leave off at a *point of interest*—one where it will be reasonably pleasant to pick the subject up again.

Use the last 5 minutes of your study session to *recall* what you have studied and to check through it once more. (This is often the *most vital part* of study, and we'll be discussing it further in the next chapter.)

So, a study session of one hour might begin with ——— minutes spent reviewing the previous work, have between ——— and ——— minutes break somewhere in the middle, and wind up with about ——— minutes review of the session's work.

5   5   10   5

2.30 So you should now be able to plan a study timetable, find a suitable place to work, and decide exactly what results you want from each study session and how to achieve them.

NB. Before going any further, pause a moment to *note* down the main points you *remember* from this chapter.

Then go on to frame 2.31.

Review Questions

The questions in the following frames should help refresh your memory. If you are unsure of an answer you can look back to the frames mentioned after the question.

2.31 How many hours have I suggested you spend on study (private sessions plus classes) in a normal week? (Frames 4–5)

40 at least

2.32 To make sure of reaching your quota of study hours and getting good value from them, you should plan out a study —— for the week ahead. (Frames 6–14)

timetable

2.33 What do *you* regard as the minimum length of time for a useful study session? (Frames 6–7)

You should be able to make effective use of an hour or even less, provided you have a plan for the session.

2.34 Each session on your weekly timetable should be allocated not just to 'study' but to (*what?*). (Frames 7–8)

a particular subject

2.35 For what kind of class period would you plan a study session . . .
1. just *after?*
2. just *before?* (Frames 9–10)

1. lecture   2. discussion

2.36 How often should you look at your timetable once you
have produced it?
a. Never again, or
b. Once a week, or
c. Once a day, or
d. Several times a day. (Frames 15–16)

d. *Several times a day.*

2.37 Every morning you should look at your timetable to
check which subjects you will be studying when. To make
sure of getting worthwhile results from these study
sessions you should then write out a list of (*what?*).
(Frames 16–17)

a list of study jobs to be done that day.

2.38 Here is one student's list of jobs to be done. Which of
them would you expect him to be able to get on with (a)
most, and (b) *least* effectively? Why? (Frames 16
and 22–23)
1. Spend the morning on meteorology.
2. Write history essay from draft outline.
3. Revise for exams.

a 2.   b 3.

Number 2 is the most clear and specific description of a
job to be done; number 3 is the vaguest.

2.39 What is the best way of getting started on a study
session? (Frames 26–27)

Begin work straight *away* (*perhaps by reviewing what you did last time*).

2.40 How can you train yourself to keep concentrating? (There are three ways at least.) (Frames 28–29)

Work for short periods but with a very definite aim. Watch out for day-dreaming and stop it at once. Take definite breaks. Make notes. (You may have thought of yet other methods.)

2.41 What is a good way to round off your study session? (Frames 29–30)

Try to recall what you have learned, or check *through what you have accomplished in the session.*

2.42 In the next chapter we'll be discussing a strategy that will help you with a job that must occupy many of your study sessions—how to get information from a textbook or article.

Please go on to Chapter 3 when you are ready.

3 How to tackle a textbook

(Study time: about 55 min)

===

3.1 Whatever else you do with your study time, you are
bound to spend a lot of it on books and articles, trying
to extract, and organise for your own purpose, the ideas
they put forward. But you need to be selective in this
reading. At the start of a course you may be presented
with a reading-list as long as your arm, and if you try to
plough sentence-by-sentence through everything on it
you'll find new titles are being added faster than you can
cross the old ones off.

Clearly, you just haven't got time to read everything;
and each text you do tackle will need to be approached
differently according to what you hope to get from it.
Remember what Francis Bacon wrote 350 years ago:

'Some books are to be tasted, others to be swallowed and
some few to be chewed and digested; that is, some books are
to be read only in parts, others to be read but not curiously
(i.e. not carefully), and some few to be read wholly and with
diligence and attention.'

Bacon describes (*how many?*) different ways of
approaching a text.

===

three

3.2 Bacon's three approaches to a text (whether book or
article) are just as useful today:
a. *tasting:* referring to isolated passages of the text.
b. *swallowing:* skimming lightly and rapidly through the
   whole text.

c. *chewing & digesting:* studying the whole text carefully with close attention.

   To choose the best way of tackling any particular book, you need only ask yourself what you hope to get out of it. Do you wish, for instance, to:
1. Get a broad, overall picture of a subject?
2. Gain a detailed, organised knowledge of all the essential facts and ideas of the subject?
3. Check on a reference/answer a specific research question?

Which of Bacon's three approaches (a, b, or c) would you consider most appropriate for each of these three different purposes in reading?

I would choose b *for purpose 1,* c *for purpose 2, and* a *for purpose 3.* Do you agree?

3.3 So, when tackling books and articles, your strategy should be flexible: you should be ready to read skimmingly or with close attention, in full or in parts, according to what you are looking for. One strategy that has proved very successful and can be adapted to most kinds of reading is often known as

SQ3R

This stands for the initial letters of the *five* steps in studying a book (or chapter, or article):
Survey
Question
Read
Recall
Review

According to this formula, the student should:

1. Get the general drift of what he is to study by carrying out a preliminary —— of the text.
2. Ask himself ——s that he expects to have answered by the time he has finished reading the text.
3. —— the text.
4. Try to —— the main points.
5. Go back and —— the text to check how well he has picked out the main points.

1. *survey*   2. *question*   3. *read*   4. *recall*   5. *review*
(Say this over to yourself a few times so as to get the sequence into your head.)

3·4 This SQ3R approach has helped bring success to thousands of students, and it is well worth thinking about in detail. Let's take it step by step:

Survey

So many of us, when we study a printed text, will 'begin at the beginning, go on until the end, and then stop.' This, however, is a useless way to read. We don't know where we are going, and we soon get so bogged down in detail that we can't see the wood for the trees. Instead, we should try to get a bird's-eye-view of the wood before we begin trampling through the undergrowth. We should *survey the whole* before we try to understand the parts.

Making a preliminary —— of a book or article, before you begin to read is like planning out your route on a —— before you begin on a difficult journey.

Surveying a Book

3.5 All books and articles are written to some kind of *plan*.
A quick survey can give you a very good idea of what
this plan is, and will therefore help you read with better
understanding.

Title page. Start your survey with the title page. You may
think you won't get much from it, but it's always worth
a glance. It can tell you:
1. The general subject area—(the title itself).
2. The level or approach—(subtitle or descriptive phrase).
3. The author's name and qualifications—(degrees, posts).
4. The date of publication—(on the back of the page).

How much of this information can you get from the
title page of the book you are looking at *now*? Please turn
to the front (if you didn't do so earlier) and take a look.

The title page tells you that this book is about studying, *that
it is merely an* introduction *to study techniques, and (very
important) that it is* programmed. *It also tells you the name
of the* author, *indicates the* experience *out of which the book
has arisen, and tells you (on the reverse side) how* recent
the book is.

3.6 So much for your 5-second analysis of the title-page.
What next?

Preface. Whether it goes by the name of Preface,
Foreword, Author's Remarks, Introduction, or whatever,
far too few people ever read the bit at the front—usually
just a few paragraphs—in which the author talks about
his book and why he wrote it. Like the title-page, this
information can help you decide whether the book is
worth your reading, and even *how* you might set about it.

Look back at the Preface to *this* book, for example. It
consists of four paragraphs followed by a final

'programmed' section, each giving you a different kind of information. (For instance, the first paragraph tells you *who* the book is intended for.)

What kind of information is given by each of the other paragraphs and by the final section of my Preface?

3.7 The four paragraphs and final section of my Preface contain information on:
1. *Who the book is written for.*
2. *Why it is necessary.*
3. *The scope and purpose of the book.*
4. *The outline and structure of the book.*
5. *How to use the book.*

Table of Contents. This again is a page (or more) of information that you should never ignore when making your preliminary survey. The contents list tells you what topics the author is dealing with and very often gives you some idea of how he has organised them—main topics, sub-topics, and so on.

Look back at the contents table for *this* book:
1. Of the following possible topics for a book about study, which are *not* given a chapter of their own?
>   essay-writing
>   note-making
>   studying a textbook
>   reading
>   discussions
>   lectures
>   psychology of study
>   organising study time
>   choosing a course
>   the need to learn study techniques
>   examinations

2. In all, there are —— chapters and each one has between —— and —— sub-sections.

1. *The book does* not *contain chapters on lectures, the psychology of study, or choosing a course.*
2. *In all, there are* eight *chapters and each one has between* four *and* seven *sub-sections.*

3.8 So your survey of a contents list tells you *what* is covered by the book and, if it is sub-divided, may give some clue as to *how* the topics are related to one another. Later, as you read through the chapters, you should *return* often to check the contents again.

    If your purpose in picking up the book was simply to look up references that might help answer a *specific* question, your preliminary survey might well *end* at this point. You can see from the table of contents whether or not the book is likely to hold anything useful.

If it is, then you can turn straight to the *back* of the book where you should be able to look up your topic in an alphabetical list telling which topics occur on which pages; this list is called an —— .

_____

index (Does this book have one?)

3.9 If you were simply looking for specific references, the index would save you a lot of time by directing you at once to the most useful passages. As the newspaper columnist, Robert Lynd, once said 'I hate reading a book without an index: it makes me read the whole book'.

    If, however, you do decide the whole book is worth 'chewing and digesting' (or even a complete chapter), take one last step in your general survey:

Leaf through the book. Run fairly quickly through the pages of the book from front to back. While leafing through:
1. Read the chapter and section headings.
2. Read the end-of-chapter summaries (if any).

3. Look at any charts and pictures.
4. Glance at the occasional sentence.

Needless to say, very little of what you see will stick in your mind at this stage. However, this quick run-through does add to what you have already guessed about the structure of the book and, like all surveying, it gets you *prepared* for the task that is to come.

Take me at my word then. Note where you have got to so far, and then leaf very quickly through the rest of *this* book to get a *general impression* of its contents. (Follow the four suggestions given above.)

Well you should now know where you are going and what sort of journey you are likely to have. (At the very least you should have noticed that three of the chapters are not written in programmed form like those you have read so far.)

3.10 So, I have suggested that when you first approach a book you should start with a general survey.
To do this you must:
1. Read the ——— page.
2. Read the author's remarks, or ———
3. Read the table of ———
4. Leaf quickly through the entire ———
5. How long do you think you might need to spend on this overall survey? Between ——— and ——— minutes.

---

1. *title*
2. *preface (or introduction, etc.)*
3. *contents*
4. *book*
5. *I asked your opinion of how long should be spent on the overall survey. Of course, it must depend on how big the text is and how important it is likely to be to you. My own feeling is that you'll need at least 5 minutes to do a worthwhile survey but probably not more than 30 minutes even if the book is to be the backbone of your course.*

3.11 Very well, you've invested a fair bit of time in surveying the whole book, for you expect to reap the dividends when you actually come to reading it. Do you, therefore, now start to read, sentence by sentence, from the beginning of Chapter One? No, you do not. You need to spend a couple more minutes at the survey stage. In fact:

Now you have completed your general survey of the book as a whole, you should do a more detailed survey of the first ——.

chapter

Surveying a Chapter

3.12 Before you begin *each* new chapter you should survey it —rather *more carefully* than you did when getting an idea of the book as a whole. Pay special attention to:

First and last paragraphs. The author may use them to give his survey of what is to come, or a summary of what he has said.

Summaries. These may appear at intervals, during the chapter as well as at the end.

Headings. Most authors have been to considerable trouble to organise their ideas under a helpful system of headings and sub-headings. Sad to say, many students completely ignore the headings, and the vital clues contained in them; they try to read a highly structured text as though it were a novel.

Obviously, headings tell you *what* topic is dealt with in each section or sub-section. But there's more to them than that. For instance:

What can you tell from the *relative sizes* or prominence of headings? (Look, for example, at the four headings on this frame.)

The relative sizes of the headings tell you how the topics are related to one another—how they go together and which comes under which.

3.13 You must be aware of the *grades* of headings in whatever you are reading. Since they tell you which topics belong with which, they are the key to the author's *structure of ideas*.

Most textbooks will use two or three grades of heading, the type decreasing in size and prominence from chapter-heading to section-heading to sub-section-heading and so on. (Thus the *difference* in prominence among the headings on the previous frame told you that it dealt with three aspects of the topic mentioned in the main heading there.)

How many *grades* of headings have I used in this chapter so far? (Note how they show up the relationships between my topics.)

Apart from the main title of the chapter, I have used three grades of heading. Here are the actual headings again, arranged to show the relationship between the topics dealt with in their sections:

3.14 Grade 1   Survey

Grade 2 **Surveying a Book**   **Surveying a Chapter**

Grade 3 *Title page*   *First and last paragraphs*
          Preface   *Summaries*
          Table of Contents   *Headings*
          Leaf through the book

You might like to finish this survey by examining the remaining headings in the chapter.

Once your survey of a chapter is complete, you are ready to move on to the second stage on the SQ3R method, which is ——.

Question (The second step of the SQ3R approach—survey, *question*, read, recall, review.)

Question

3.15 Never begin the detailed reading of a text without having in mind a set of questions that you want answered. Questions are a great simulus to learning for they give you a sense of *purpose* and keep you alert. You become an active researcher rather than a passive browser.

Where do the questions come from? The main source is you:

One of the benefits of making a preliminary —— of a book or chapter is that it gives you the chance to think up some relevant ——s.

---

survey   question

Your Own Questions

3.16 In surveying the book as a whole, your questions are likely to be pretty general ones. Glancing at the title-page, preface, and table of contents, for instance, you might ask yourself:
'How far can I trust this book, published five years ago?'
'Will it be as helpful to *me* as its preface suggests?'
'Why does the author think it worth giving a whole chapter to such-and-such a topic?'

Even these *general* questions are of some help to you in deciding how to treat the book.

But when you turn from surveying the book as a whole to surveying the chapter you are about to read, your questions will become much (*more/less?*) specific.

---

more

3.17 *Headings* and sub-headings of sections should always bring questions into your mind. For instance, when you saw the heading 'Question' a couple of frames ago, you might have asked:
'Why has the author used this as a heading? Who questions whom? What part do questions play in study? Where do they come from? How do I find the answers?' and so on.
Some of these questions are already answered, others soon will be.

Look at the next three headings (on frames 3.19, 3.20 and 3.23). What *questions* do they bring to your mind?

'Other people's questions' might lead you to ask: 'Which other people? Students? Authors? Tutors? Are their questions as useful as my own? Where do I find the answers?' and so on.

'Questions in programmed learning' might prompt: 'What is programmed learning? What do such questions have to do with study? What use are they? What sort of questions?' and so on.

'Read' might suggest: 'Don't I know how to do this already? Do I have to learn new ways? What does he say here that is not in the chapter on reading?' and so on.

3.18 So *headings* should be a very fruitful source of questions— questions that give you a sense of purpose. You should be able to take practically any heading and pull at least one question out of it, if only 'What does it mean?'

Questions should also come to mind as you look at the *first and last paragraphs*, and at any *summaries*. For example:
'Where are the facts to back up these statements? Can I be mistaken in what I thought I knew about this subject? Have I met these technical terms before?' and so on.

Are you (as the reader) the *only* source of questions?

No. (As you should remember from your survey of the following heading!)

Other People's Questions

3.19 Sometimes your *tutor* may suggest questions to bear in mind while reading a particular chapter. Or your *colleagues* may pose questions (or offer comments that are easily re-phrased as comments) about chapters they have had to struggle with.

But perhaps the most useful outside source of questions can be the book itself. The *author* will often pose three or four questions at the beginning of a chapter, and their answers should have become apparent to you by the time you reach the end.

Sometimes authors give you a list of questions at the *end* of a chapter. Since questions are generally more helpful if posed at the *start* of a reading session, you should:

Take note of these end-of-chapter questions during your preliminary —— of the chapter, and then consider them again after you have finished —— ing it.

3.20 Unfortunately, students too often take no notice of the author's questions and thereby pass up a very helpful guide to study.

Questions in programmed learning. In a programmed book (like this one) questions play an essential part in the flow of the argument, and you can learn a lot about how to read from the way programmes are written.

The author of a programme asks questions of many kinds (direct, multiple-choice, fill-in-the-blanks) but his purpose is always the same—to draw your attention to the most important point he is putting across and make you respond to it.

And your response to the question helps you to ——— .

───

learn (or understand).

3.21 Programmes are a fast and effective way of learning and, gradually, more and more material is appearing in this form. There are programmes in many school subjects (particularly Maths, Science, and English Grammar) and an increasing number at college level.

But programmes can teach you something almost more valuable than the subject-matter they contain. That is, they can get you into the habit of *reading questioningly*.

In a sense, you should mentally 'programme' everything you read. Be constantly asking yourself questions: 'What is the *most crucial idea* in this chapter? This section? This paragraph?'

Questions like 'How? When? Who? Where? and (especially) So What? should rarely be out of your thoughts as you read. And as one question is answered, another should arise.

Normally the answers to your questions will emerge from the text as you read on. What action might you take if an important question is *not* answered in the ensuing text?

Well, if it was an important question you might feel inclined to make a note of it and seek the answer elsewhere—from a tutor, a colleague, another book, etc.

3.22 So, one of the most important reasons for making a preliminary survey is that you get a chance to raise a few questions that will give purpose to your reading. At first you may find question-raising difficult but, with practice, you will soon do it automatically. If you read questioningly, the questions will come.

Having made your *survey* and started to *question* you are now ready for the third step in the SQ3R approach which is to —— the text.

---

read

Read

3.23 So reading is the third step in studying a book, *not* (as many students appear to think) the first and only step.

Now what kind of reading is called for? Certainly not the kind that most people use with fiction—in an attempt to 'take one's mind off things'. Your purpose is the very reverse of this: you are trying to *apply* your mind, with all its critical skills.

In fact, as we have just decided, you must read *actively*—in search of *answers*. Remember:

The reader with a —— to be answered is a reader with a *purpose*.

Look for the Main Idea

3.24 Perhaps the most purposeful question you can ask yourself is, as I've suggested before, 'What is the *main idea?*' Main ideas can be found at each level of the book. The book as a whole will have, perhaps, one very general main idea. The main idea of each chapter will be rather less general. Each section within a chapter will have a more specific main idea, and the main idea of each paragraph will be most specific of all. Your job is to pick out the main idea *at each level*. Let's try this: Below are four *main ideas* from the book you are reading now:

a. 'One effective study technique is the SQ3R approach.'
b. 'The chief aim in reading should be to find the main ideas.'
c. 'The reading step in SQ3R must be active and purposeful.'
d. 'Most students would benefit from more effective study techniques.'

Which of these main ideas belongs to:
1. the book as a whole?
2. this chapter of the book?
3. this section (headed 'Read')?
4. the paragraph above (starting 'Perhaps')?
Write down your answers, then turn to frame 3.25.

1. *d*   2. *a*   3. *c*   4. *b*

3.25 *The author's plan.* If you read a book critically, you should
be able to detect its hierarchy of ideas—the author's plan
whereby the main idea of the *book* (level 1) *breaks down*
into a number of more specific main ideas each of which
is the theme of a *chapter* (level 2), and each chapter
main idea breaks down to provide main ideas for each
of its *sections* (level 3), and each section idea provides
even more specific main ideas, one for each paragraph
(level 4).

   This diagram could illustrate the hierarchy of ideas
(each disc a main idea) for a small book or pamphlet:

In your *surveys*, you will probably have grasped the main
ideas at levels —— and ——, and perhaps at level
—— also; at the *read* step of SQ3R you will be
concerned chiefly with the main ideas at level ——.

1   2   3   4
(At the *read* step of SQ3R you'll need to pick out the main idea from each *paragraph*.)

Two Don'ts

3.26 Do *not* attempt to make notes during the *read* step. To do so can be distracting and it slows you down. Also, it produces the temptation to note the author's words rather than your own, and this is no help at all to understanding and learning.

Do *not* underline words or phrases, either—not on *first* reading. Although it might give you a feeling of being active, you'd too often find, on reflection, that you'd underlined the wrong things.

So, on first reading, you should look for the ——— ——s, but should neither ——— bits of the text nor make ——s.

_____

main ideas   *underline*   *notes*

Read It Again

3.27 Many students find it useful to read the text *twice* at this step in SQ3R. Here is what they would advise.
1. Read straight through the material concentrating on the *main ideas*. Don't stop to underline or take notes. Just put quick check marks in the margin with pencil whenever you see an important idea. (Or, if the book does not belong to you, put slips of paper in the book.)
2. Read through a second time, confirming that you really have picked out the main ideas, but this time paying rather more attention than before to the *supporting detail*. Underline the main idea in each paragraph and any important details. (But only, of course, if the book belongs to you.)

So, having done your preliminary ——s and asked yourself ——s, you have —— the text *twice* and have marked its —— ideas. You are now ready to take the fourth step in SQ3R by trying to —— what you have studied.

surveys   questions   read   main   recall

Recall

3.28 The business of studying a text does not finish with reading even if the material is perfectly straightforward. For instance you have presumably had no difficulty in *understanding* the ideas you've read in this programme.

Does this mean you will be able to bring them all back to mind, say a week from now?

Almost certainly not, *unless you are gifted with an exceptional memory. Most people forget 50 per cent of what they read within* seconds *of putting down a book—except when they make an* active *attempt to recall.*

The Value of Recall

3.29 Make regular attempts to recall and you'll improve your learning in three ways:
1. You'll *concentrate* better because you'll know you have the task awaiting you.
2. You'll have the chance to *remedy* any lapses of memory or misunderstandings.
3. You'll be kept *active* because you must come to grips with what you have read and summarise it in your own words.

Could you get all these benefits simply by going back and *reading through the text once again?*

No, *a re-reading is no substitute for recall.* (*As you surely know, the fact that you can* recognise *ideas once you see them again is no proof that you can* remember *them without the book in front of you, let alone put them into your own words.*)

How Often to Recall?

3.30 Once you have started reading, then, you should *pause* frequently and *tell yourself the main points* you have read. Sometimes it will be sufficient to stop at the end of every chapter and recall.

But usually, unless the chapter is very short, you'd be wise to recall *also* at the end of every . . .

    sentence?   **A**
    paragraph? **B**
    section?   **C**

_____

3.31 **A.** *Unless you were reading extraordinarily long sentences, you would not be wise to try recalling at the end of each one you read. To do so would make your learning too bitty, and you would probably lose sight of, or never see, the main ideas. You'll need to take rather larger bites at the material if you want to get it organised in your mind. Please return to frame 3.30 and re-consider your answer.*

B. *With an exceptionally long or involved paragraph it may sometimes be worth looking away from your book a moment to see if you can summarise that paragraph in your mind. But it would not be wise to get into the habit of stopping after every* *paragraph (or even couple of paragraphs) since this might prevent you from following the flow of the author's argument. Please read paragraph C below.*

C. *If you waited until the end of a long chapter you might already have forgotten so much that your recall would be far too hazy. But to recall at the end of every sentence or paragraph would make your learning weak and disjointed. The best plan, then, is to go for a section at a time. Every time you see a new* main heading *come up, stop and recall the chapter so far.*

Then recall *again*, covering *all* the sections this time, when you get right to the end of the ——— . Go to frame 3.32.

chapter

Make Notes

3.32 Don't just *think* your recall. *Write down* the key points you remember. Make brief *notes* of the main ideas and any details you think important.
Even the sketchiest note-making is far more valuable than simply allowing half-formed memories to drift through your mind. It is easy to be *over-confident* about how much one remembers—until one tries to pin it down in words. (Besides, you need a *record* of what you have read. More about this in Chapter 6.)

So you should start making notes as part of the ——— step in the SQ3R approach.

How Much Time on Recall?

3.33 Quite a sizeable chunk of your SQ3R time should be spent on the *recall* step. As an example, consider the reasonably well-organised and meaningful material you are likely to meet in courses on education, psychology, economics, or geography: here perhaps 50 per cent of your study time should be spent recalling what you have read.

Taking this as a measure, would you expect to have to spend *more* or *less* than 50 per cent of your time recalling:

1. Material that has to be learned
   by heart, e.g. rules, symbols,
   names, laws, formulae? —— than 50 per cent.

2. History, philosophy, literature,
   biography, and any material
   with a 'story-like' content? —— than 50 per cent.

---

1. *probably* more *than 50 per cent (perhaps as much as 90 per cent)*
2. *probably* less *than 50 per cent (maybe only 20 per cent)*

3.34 So be prepared to spend *half* your study time recalling what you have read (and even more if the material is difficult to remember). Experiments have proved that this is not time wasted. In fact, the time-wasters are those people whose aim is simply to 'get one more book out of the way'. Even if they understand while they read, they will soon forget.

Having made notes of what you recall, you are now ready for the fifth and final step of SQ3R: you —— everything you have done so far.

Review

3.35 Here your purpose is to check the truth of your recall. Never try to convince yourself that you remember everything correctly: always *view again* to make sure.

How to Review

Your best line of action is to do a quick *repeat* of the previous four steps:

1. *Survey* the general structure of the section or chapter. (Look again at the headings and any summaries.)
2. Remind yourself of the *questions* you asked. Can you answer them all? Do any new questions arise?
3. *Re-read* the text to see that you've remembered everything of importance.
4. Complete your *recall* by filling any holes and correcting any faults in your notes.

Try this now with the chapter so far:

First *recall* the headings and the main points, making some brief *notes* from memory.
Then follow the four steps of *review* to check how well you have remembered.

How well did you do? Better than you normally expect to, I hope. (But not as well as if you'd tried to recall after *each* of the five sections.)

3.36 The five steps of SQ3R have been tried out by thousands of college students, who have reported very favourably on the increased effectiveness with which they have come to study. Almost certainly you too could benefit from the same approach. You might need to *bend it and adapt it*, or alter the balance or the timing of its steps, to suit your individual needs, but the basic strategy is *flexible* enough for you to use it many different ways and still get good results.

Suppose three different students were to offer the three different views of SQ3R that I describe below. Which view would you think most *practical*?

'It doesn't matter in what order you take the steps as long as you don't miss any out or try to take two steps at once.'   **A**

'The steps will overlap to some extent and an early step may even need to be repeated later in the sequence.'   **B**

'Each step must be completely finished before the next one can begin.'   **C**

3.37 **A.** *I'm not sure how practical (or even possible) it would be to recall before you had read, or review before you had surveyed, so the order of steps in SQ3R is surely the logical one. Certainly it would be unwise to leave out any of the steps, but as for taking two at once. . . . Please read paragraph B below.*

B. *Although the steps of SQ3R are in the natural, logical order and should therefore be followed, we must expect some overlap and repetition between them. For instance, even while the emphasis is on survey or read, we may still be asking questions; or we may want to interrupt the read step in order to recall and review or to repeat our survey of the text.*

SQ3R gives you a flexible approach that can be varied according to your purpose and the kind of material you are studying. Please go on to frame 3.38.

C. *When you come to apply the SQ3R technique in practice you will find it difficult to stop asking questions once you reach the read step, to avoid reading when you come to review, and so on. Please read paragraph B above before you continue.*

3.38 There is one final question we ought to consider before winding up this chapter:

So far we've talked about the SQ3R approach only in relation to *texts:* books, reports, articles, etc.
Do you think *any or all* of the five steps could be applied to the kind of studying you do in a *lecture?*
If so: *Which* steps? *How* would you apply them?

Compare your judgement with mine:
1. *Survey.* Difficult to apply to a lecture unless the lecturer himself is prepared to tell you where he is heading. Some are, however, and it is always worth asking.
2. *Question.* Preliminary questioning may be difficult without the co-operation of the lecturer, but even so you should be able to think up general questions as soon as you know of the subject, and you should certainly be able to *listen questioningly* once he has begun to speak.
3. *Read.* Impossible unless he provides you with a copy of his notes, but of course *listen* serves exactly the same function.
4. *Recall.* Entirely practicable, and even more *essential* than it is with books.
5. *Review.* Possible in so far as you can check what you recall against what other people thought they heard. And if there are points you still aren't sure about, you can ask the lecturer.

3.39 So, to a large extent, the SQ3R approach is applicable to lectures as well as books. Try it anyway: it's such a powerful technique that it can adapt itself to give *some* help in almost any job of study (even field work, laboratory work, tutorials, and so on). Certainly you should be able to adapt it to tackle any films, sound-recordings or television programmes that form part of your course.

In the next chapter you have a chance to apply SQ3R to a real text. But, first check through the following review questions which should remind you of some of the main ideas in this chapter.

Review Questions

(If any question gives you difficulty, turn back to the appropriate frames.)

3.40 List in order the five steps of SQ3R. (Frames 3–4)

Survey   question   read   recall   review

3.41 What steps might you take in surveying a book *as a whole?* (Frames 5–11)

Read the title-page, the preface, and the table of contents (together perhaps with the index); and leaf quickly through the book.

3.42 Before reading an article or a particular chapter within a textbook, it is necessary to survey it in rather more detail. What are the *three* things you would look at in surveying a chapter? (Frames 12–14)

First and last paragraphs, summaries, and headings.

3.43 At what steps of SQ3R should you be asking questions? (Frames 16–22)

Mainly at the question *step (which tends to mingle with the* survey *and the* read *step), but also during* recall *and* review. *In fact, questions should arise at* all *steps.*

3.44 In tackling a textbook you have to sort out the *main ideas* at all levels from the book, to the chapter, to the section, to the paragraph. At the *read* step you will be chiefly concerned with the main ideas at *which level?* (Frames 25–26)

3.45 There are *two* things which you should *avoid* doing on *first reading* of a text. *What* are they? *Why* avoid them? (Frame 26)

Do not make notes or underline. (While reading you would be too likely to use the author's words instead of your own, and on first reading you might well underline the wrong things.)

3.46 At what points should you *recall* during your study of a textbook? (Frames 30–31)

At least at the end of every chapter, and most probably at the end of every section within the chapter as well.

3.47 What should you do at the *recall* step? (Frame 32)

Write down the main things you remember.

3.48 Why is it necessary to *review*? What should you do at the review step? (Frame 35)

To check the truth of your recall:
Remind yourself of your survey and the questions you asked, re-read the text, and complete your recall by polishing up your notes.

3.49 Now the next chapter is unprogrammed, so as to give you the chance to apply SQ3R to some normal text material. (I would suggest you *recall* between four and six times on your way through.)

Please go on to make your preliminary *survey* of Chapter 4.

4 How to write essays

(Study time: about 25 min)

The Value of Essays

For many students essay-writing is the bane of their lives.
They question the usefulness of essays, make heavy
weather of writing them, and generally try to put off the
task for as long as they can get away with it.

This is most unfortunate, for the writing of an essay
can help the student in three ways:

1. It forces him to organise his thinking and come up
   with his own point of view on a topic.
2. It enables him (and his tutor) to recognise strengths
   that he must build on and weaknesses that he must
   remedy if he is to succeed in his course.
3. It gives him practice that will be useful in examinations
   (since most examinations still call for the ability to
   write essays).

Of these three benefits, perhaps the greatest is the
first. After we've read, heard and talked about a topic,
our minds are awash with ideas and impressions. But we
never really get to grips with this experience unless we
try to write it down. It is only when we come to put
words on paper that we are forced to make these ideas
precise, weigh them up, reject those that are irrelevant,
and organise the rest into a sensible pattern that we can
call our own. *Writing is the crucial step* without which the
process of study is incomplete. (And since practically
every occupation you might enter will demand the same
ability to report in writing, it is clearly a 'life-skill'.)

Understanding the Task

Many difficulties in writing an essay arise because the student has not planned it carefully enough or has not really thought about what the essay requires of him. He is only interested in getting it out of the way as quickly as possible.

When your tutor gives you an essay theme or title, take it down exactly, and examine the *precise* wording: what is demanded of you? Does the question or title call for a general treatment or for specific cases, a broad outline or a detailed account? Are you expected to state your own personal experience and opinions or simply to demonstrate your knowledge of other people's? Are you asked to refer to any particular sources of information or experimental data? Are you expected merely to describe things as they are (or were) or must you analyse and explain why they came to be that way? Need you discuss implications and suggest applications?

Collecting Your Material

Once you have decided on the nature and scope of the essay you have to write, it is time to do some research into its subject-matter. Normally, you will need to go to a variety of sources for the material out of which you will shape your essay.

Questions

Whatever you do, don't just grab a pile of books and begin reading in the vague hope that something useful will pop out. Such browsing would be a waste of your precious time. To get results you must read *purposefully*, and the best way of ensuring this (as I've said before) is to have a set of specific questions that you want answered.

Now obviously you'll have an essay question (or title) but this is too broad—it needs breaking down before you can begin any useful research. The best way of breaking it down is to ask yourself questions about it. These questions can then guide you in your reading.

For instance, suppose you were asked to write on 'The Use of Programmed Learning in Education and Industrial Training'. You might begin by analysing the title and coming up with a set of questions like these:

1. What is programmed learning? How long has it been in use?
2. Who uses it most, education or industry? Why?
3. Do they use it in similar ways or differently? Why?
4. How does it compare with other forms of learning? What sort of results does it get? What do students think of it? Are there any difficulties attached to using it?
5. Will it be more used or less in the future? Will it be used in new ways? Will even newer methods take its place?

And so on.

Always try to think out (and write down) a few questions in this way before you begin your research for an essay. As you read, you will come up with further questions, more specific questions, and perhaps some of those on your original list will seem less relevant; but to have at least some questions to answer, right from the start, is an invaluable aid in research. The more clearly you know what information you are looking for, the more effectively you will read. So you'll save yourself a good deal of time.

Start Early

Start doing this preliminary thinking, and writing down your research questions, as early as possible after hearing the title of your essay. Even if a tutor gives you a month or more, do some thinking right away: don't wait until the week before your deadline.

There are two very good reasons for at least making a start immediately:

1. In classes or in casual conversation, and especially in your general study reading, you may quite accidentally come across ideas that will be relevant to your essay. If you have not already given some thought to your essay topic, you may miss many of these ideas and end up having to re-read the texts merely because you didn't realise their significance the first time.

2. We all know how often we get a brilliant idea on a topic at a moment when we are thinking about something entirely different. The unconscious mind seems to go on chewing away at a problem even though we have turned our attention to other matters. So the more time you can leave between your first thinking about your essay and the day when you finally write it up, the more chance you are giving your unconscious mind to throw up new ideas and discover new relationships.

Keep a Notebook

It is wise to keep some sort of notebook with a page or so devoted to each essay or project that you have on the stocks at any one time. Then, if an idea occurs to you, or if you come across a useful quotation or illustration, or if you think of a piece of research to be followed up later, you can fasten it down on paper before it fades from the memory. Many successful students (and authors) claim they owe much of their success to the habit of always having such a book in their pockets and never letting a good idea escape unrecorded.

Sources of Information

Now where do you start looking for the answers to your research questions—the answers that will help you shape up your essay? Your major source of ideas is likely to lie in *reading*.

Possibly your tutor, when he sets the essay topic, will give you a basic list of books and periodicals. And when you begin looking at texts from this bibliography you will probably find that they in turn suggest further books and articles that might be helpful to you. You may get useful ideas from textbooks, biographies, reference books and encyclopedias, research papers, learned journals, government reports, newspaper cuttings, and so on. If you have trouble tracking down the right references your college library staff will be glad to advise you. (Do ask them to explain the library's system and resources—one of the most valuable things you can learn in college is how to make best use of a library.)

Don't neglect the less formal sources of information, however. While the essay plan is hatching out in your mind you should be alert for useful ideas that crop up unexpectedly in lectures, seminars and tutorials, in your own personal experience, and in casual discussions with fellow-students or with tutors.

Record Your Sources

Whatever the source of your ideas, do make note of where you get them from. In writing down any idea that you think may have a bearing on your essay, record the title and author of the book or article (and who published it, when and where), or the name of the speaker, from whom you heard it. You *must* give credit to these sources if you use them in your essay. It creates a very bad impression with your tutor if, through carelessness or lapse of memory, you later present him with ideas as if they were your own but which he recognises as coming from other authors (especially if he is one of them!).

Planning the Essay

Never jump straight from research into writing the first sentence of your essay. Too many essays start off in a flurry of enthusiasm only to fizzle out a few paragraphs later through lack of a sense of direction. Think your essay right through before you write a word. That is, make a *plan*.

Selection of Material

The first step in planning is to weigh up, and select from, the material you have collected in your research. You may have pages of notes. Which of them are relevant? Do avoid the amateurish habit of trying to 'work them all in somehow'. Not all your ideas will be equally useful when you get down to shaping your essay. Some will seem trivial. Others will seem obscure. Yet others will be unsupported by sufficient evidence. These must be discarded. You will have no space for waffle, padding, or half-truths.

At the same time, remember that you will need examples to back up any statements of fact or opinion that you'll be making in your essay. Such material is not padding; indeed it is vital to the credibility and strength of your argument. Also, be sure that you have enough material to give due weight to *all* aspects of the essay. (Students often ignore the 'reasons' or 'implications' they were asked to discuss.)

What you must do is *select* just the most appropriate material for your essay, enough to cover it fully but not too much to confuse the issue. Having done this, and once you are sure of your facts and your sources, you can start arranging your ideas logically so as to make the greatest impact in your essay.

Write an Outline

The next step in planning your essay is to work out the basic structure or *outline*. Doing this has several advantages:
1. It helps you sort out what are the main ideas and the important details.

2. It makes sure you leave out nothing vital and that you don't repeat yourself.

3. It allows you, once started, to write fluently without having to keep chewing your pen and wondering what to say next.

4. If you are in an examination and time runs out on you, you may well gain more marks from submitting a clear outline than you would from a half-finished essay.

A basic framework. Here is a 3-point plan that you may have used before but which still is useful as a framework for a wide variety of essays:

1. *Introduction*
   A. Comment on subject of essay. (What do you understand by it? How is it important? etc.)
   B. Which aspects you will deal with and why. (Remember you can't say everything about anything in just a thousand words or so.)

2. *The Main Body*
   A. Develop your line of argument through three or four main ideas.
   B. Support each main idea with examples and illustrations drawn from experience or other authors.

3. *Conclusion*
   A. Summary of main ideas.
   B. Firm or tentative answer to question; or comment on topic of essay, indicating wider implications or future trends, or scope for further consideration.

I have already suggested (frame 3.25) that your job in reading should be to uncover the writer's outline of ideas (as I hope you are now uncovering *my* outline for this chapter). Before writing, of course, your job is just the opposite—to plan an outline for your own ideas. (One useful form of outline is shown on frame 7.8: please look at it now.)

Start at the End

With a carefully planned outline and the notes you have made from your research, you should be able to start writing your essay. However, many students would suggest taking one final step in the planning: they would advise you to write the *last* paragraph of your essay first. We can justify this on two grounds:

1. It gives a sense of direction to your writing if you know exactly what conclusion you're heading towards.
2. It helps ensure that your essay will conclude firmly and definitely, rather than just stopping lamely as so many do.

Perhaps you can summarise the theme of your essay in just one sentence: for example, 'Programmed learning is still in its infancy and, while at present used more in industry than in education, its benefits are bringing it rapidly-growing acceptance in both fields'. If you can write such a summary sentence, then you could use it as the topic sentence of your final paragraph.

Writing the Essay

Having selected the important ideas, made an outline, and written your final paragraph, you can begin writing your essay. But regard this as your first, trial draft. As one writer once said: 'The best reason for putting anything down on paper is that one may then change it.' Write as well as you can, but be prepared to make changes later. At this stage you should be more concerned with getting your ideas down somehow than with the best possible wording. You'll know better what you want to say when you see what you've written!

Style

Style is nothing more than the words with which you choose to express your thoughts. If your thoughts are woolly and confused, then your style will be also, and your essay will be difficult to read and understand. If, on the other hand, you have a clear picture of what you are trying to say and you know exactly where your argument is leading, then you should be able to write clearly and directly in a way that is easy for a reader to follow.

It is always best to write as simply and straightforwardly as possible. Use everyday language, but avoid slang. Write short sentences. Be concise: never write a paragraph when one sentence will do the same job. A very useful guide-book to style is *The Complete Plain Words* by Sir Ernest Gowers.

Layout

Let the layout of your essay on the pages reflect the structure of your outline. If appropriate, use headings and sub-headings within your essay. Split your work up into paragraphs: each main idea should have its own paragraph. All this helps your reader with *his* task.

Remember also that a picture can save you a great many words. Where a map or diagram or graph can save you writing a description use it instead of words.

Make a clear distinction between your own ideas and those you've borrowed from other authors. Name your sources. If you are quoting other people's actual words, use quotation marks. Acknowledge any books or articles from which you have particularly drawn by writing a bibliography in the way I have done at the end of this chapter; and refer to these works by writing, for example, (Gowers, 1962) after any reference or quotation within your essay.

Re-writing

Having written your essay you should put it aside for a few days. You need this time-lapse to allow for the pride of authorship to subside. It is a great mistake to work so close to your deadline that you have no choice but to hand in the first draft as soon as it has come from your pen. Changes will almost certainly be needed.

Just a few days can give you quite a new perspective on your work. You will come back to it fresh, able to look at it more objectively, and you'll see a great many obscurities and pomposities that were not apparent to you in the heat of creation. In short, you will be able to assess it more *critically*—much as your reader will.

A Check-list

Here are some useful questions to ask yourself about it:

1. Does the essay answer the question or deal with the topic that was set?
2. Does it cover all the main aspects and in sufficient depth?
3. Is the content accurate and relevant?
4. Is the material logically arranged?
5. Is each main point well supported by examples and argument?
6. Is there a clear distinction between your ideas and those you have brought in from other authors?
7. Do you acknowledge all sources and references?
8. Is the length of the essay right for its purpose?
9. Is it written plainly and simply, without clumsy or obscure phrasing? (A good test is to *read it aloud*.)
10. Is the grammar, punctuation and spelling acceptable, and is it neatly and legibly written?

Be strict with yourself on each of these points, since these are the questions your reader will ask himself in marking the essay. *Re-write* your final draft so as to eliminate all the weaknesses you have spotted.

If you find it difficult to criticise your own work in this way, get a friend to examine your essay while you do the same for his. You will both learn from one another's comments. Teach yourself to look at your essays in the same way your reader will and you'll have gone a long way towards improving your grades.

Physical Appearance

Whatever you do, don't neglect the physical appearance of your essay. Make sure your final draft is neat, well laid-out, and either clearly-written or, preferably, *typed*. First impressions are very important in so subjective a job as marking an essay, and untidy work suggests untidy thinking. However unfair it may seem, tutors are only human, and they tend to be impatient with essays that are difficult to read: experiments have shown that bad hand-writing can cost you one whole grade in your score. It's no joke to get a B when legible writing could have earned you an A on the same essay. You have been warned!

By the way, essays do occasionally go missing after being handed in to a tutor. Carbon paper is cheap and easy insurance against the inconvenience and aggravation this might cause you. Whether you type or write by hand, always make a carbon copy of your final draft. (Or if you're rich enough to make it even easier for yourself, use a photo-copier.)

One final point: Never be too anxious to get an essay out of the way. It's probably when you are most fed up with it that you are on the verge of producing something really worthwhile. Try to look on it not as a chore to be disposed of, nor as an obstacle to be overcome, but as a means of sharpening-up your thinking and as a personal expression of how well you understand.

Bibliography

Flesch, R. (1949)   *The Art of Readable Writing*
New York: Harper

Gowers, Sir Ernest (1962)   *The Complete Plain Words*
London: Penguin

Kapp, R. O. (1948)   *The Presentation of Technical Information*
London: Constable

Maddox, H. (1963)   *How to Study* London: Pan
(Chapter 10 on 'Writing English')

4.1 Now:

1. Complete your *recall* of the chapter and make sure you have some notes. (I'll show you my own notes on the chapter as a check, later.)
2. *Review* the chapter.

Then tackle the review questions that follow.

Review Questions

4.2 (If you need to refresh your memory, turn back to the *page*-number mentioned.)

What are the *five* stages in producing an essay? (Pages 66–74)

Understanding the task, collecting the material, planning the essay, writing the essay, and re-writing it.

4.3 Before you begin your *research* for an essay you should examine the title and work out a set of ——s to guide you. (Page 66)

---

questions

4.4 If you have the title of an essay to be completed 10 weeks from now, when would be the best time to start thinking about it? Why? (Page 67)

Now. The longer the problem can simmer in your unconscious, the better; and you must be alert right away for relevant ideas that crop up in other work and may save you labour later on.

4.5 What are the steps (at least two) in *planning* an essay? (Page 69)

Selecting your material, writing an outline, and (perhaps) drafting out the final paragraph.

4.6 Would you say the *style* of the chapter you have just read would generally be suitable for writing an essay? What word would you use to describe such a style? (Page 73)

Your opinion is what I asked for. Mine is that such a style (plain, simple, direct, natural) is suitable for most essays.

4.7 If you are using the ideas or the actual words of *other* writers within your essay, what steps will you take to let your reader know this? (Page 73)

Use quotation marks, name the other authors, write a bibliography.

4.8 In *re*-writing your essay (producing the final draft) you should try to examine it from *whose* point of view? (Page 75)

From the point of view of the reader it is intended for.

4.9 Does it really make any practical difference whether or not your handwriting is clearly legible and your essay set out neatly on the page? Explain. (Page 75)

It does matter, because scruffy-looking work will almost certainly lose you marks, and it will also be more difficult for you to revise from later.

4.10 Go on to Chapter 5 (and don't forget to SURVEY it before you begin reading).

5 How to read better and faster

(Study time: about 50 min)

5.1 Most college students have been reading for a dozen years or more, yet few do it as well as they might. They read too slowly, they can't concentrate, and they don't remember what they've read. Since reading plays so large a part in a student's work, he clearly stands to gain if he can learn to do it with greater speed and comprehension.

Better Reading

The first essential is to improve *comprehension*. How can you get a better understanding of a text, and remember it once you have read it?

The best way, as we have already decided, is to apply the SQ3R method. (This will make his reading *active* and *purposeful*.)

That is, you should not begin reading a chapter until you have ——ed it, and asked ——s about it; and once you have —— it you should try to —— what you have read, and then —— it.

survey   question   read   recall   review

5.2 The effective reader is the one who is reading purposefully with questions to be answered.

NB. Have you surveyed this chapter and asked yourself questions about it yet?

In any intensive reading of a text (whether book, chapter, article, report, etc.) you will probably be trying to:

1. Find the *main ideas*.
2. Pick out *important details*.
3. *Evaluate* what you are reading.

Main Ideas

As we discussed in the chapter on SQ3R, main ideas can be found at the level of the *book*, the *chapter*, the *section*, and the *paragraph*. You will *already* have got some grasp of the more general main ideas from your preliminary survey.

At the *read* stage you will be looking chiefly for the main idea in each ——— .

═══════════════════════════════════════

paragraph

5.3 *Topic sentences*. Most writers put just one main idea in each paragraph, and your job is to find it. Usually this main idea is stated in *one* sentence—called the *topic* sentence.

Very commonly, the writer *starts* his paragraph by stating the main idea. He then illustrates it, supports it, or elaborates on it in the rest of the paragraph.

So the topic sentence is often the ——— sentence in the paragraph.

═══════════════════════════════════════

So the topic sentence is often the first *sentence in the paragraph*. (It contains the main idea.)

5.4 Sometimes, however, the writer feels it will be more effective to *lead up* to his main idea rather than start out with it. In this case, he will hold back his topic sentence until the end of the paragraph. The major point of the paragraph will come in its *final* sentence.

Which sentence carries the main idea of the paragraph above?

The first.	**A**
The second.	**B**
The last.	**C**

5.5   **A.** *The main idea there was that a paragraph may have its major point in its last sentence. Now the sentence you picked out says that a writer often prefers to lead up to his main idea. Does this necessarily mean that he leaves it till the very end of the paragraph? No, it does not; so this sentence does not carry the main idea of that paragraph. Please take another look at frame 5.4.*

B. *Almost, but not quite. The main idea there was that a paragraph may have its major point in its last sentence. The sentence you have picked out says that a writer may hold back his topic sentence until the end of a paragraph. But this doesn't necessarily mean that he makes it the very last sentence, does it? And if you look at the paragraph again, you'll see that one of its sentences openly states the main idea leaving no doubt about it. Please look at frame 5.4 again.*

C. *The paragraph you looked at begins by saying that a writer often prefers to lead up to his main idea, and that he may leave his topic sentence until the end of the paragraph. But, as you say, it is the final sentence that neatly states the main idea. Please go on to frame 5.6.*

5.6   Normally, then, the —— sentence (carrying the main idea) is either the —— or the —— in the paragraph.

5.7 Very rarely will you find the topic sentence in the middle of a paragraph. But what you will come across, from time to time, is the kind of paragraph in which no single sentence can be said to carry the main idea. Particularly in fiction, or in paragraphs of descriptive writing, the essential idea may be spread out across the whole paragraph, or never stated explicitly at all.

But in the normal textbook or article, you will expect to find the —— —— contained in the first or last sentence.

main idea

Important Details

5.8 As well as picking out the main ideas, you'll need to have your eyes open for important details. Some students complain they can find the main ideas but not the significant details. Others are so impressed by the details they can't see the main ideas. Yet others just can't tell the difference.

As I mentioned while we were discussing SQ3R, it sometimes pays to —— a chapter a *second* time in order to pick out the important details.

read

5.9 Just what is an important detail? It is one that clarifies, or supports, or illustrates, or develops the main idea. It may be an example, a proof, an explanation, an implication. Usually there is at least one important detail attached to each main idea.

Frame 5.7 has a paragraph in it. Look back now, and pick out:
1. The main idea.
2. One important detail.

---

1. *'The main idea may be spread over all the sentences in a paragraph'* (or words to that effect).
2. *'Particularly in fiction and descriptive writing'* is the only important detail—an example.

5.10 Sometimes it is a matter of *opinion* as to whether a particular detail is significant or not. Ask yourself:
Is this the best possible example (or proof, etc.) of the main idea?
Does the main idea really *need* supporting, or proving, or illuminating?
If a detail does not seem very important, you will presumably not take note of it.

Look for example at the second-to-last paragraph in Chapter 4 (Essay-writing)—the paragraph on page 75 beginning 'Whatever you do,':
1. What is the main idea?
2. What would *you* regard as important details?

---

1. *The main idea is that the physical appearance of an essay is worth taking care over.*
2. *You might well have decided any or all of these details are important enough to note:*
   a. *three aspects of 'physical appearance'—neatness, layout, legibility*
   b. *advisability of typing*
   c. *the human impatience of tutors*
   d. *experimental evidence of the effects of poor handwriting.*

5.11 *Look for signposts.* One way of spotting important details (and of confirming main ideas) is to look out for the clues that the author has used to help you read. He may have used both *visual* and *verbal* signposts.

Consider the *visual* signposts first:

1. Words printed in *italics*, or
2. Words underlined, or
3. Words in **bold face** type.
4. The *numbering* of points (as in this list).
5. The *lettering* of points (a, b, c, etc., as in the list at the top of the frame).

Which of these five kinds of clue have I used so far in this programme?

I have used all the visual signposts except underlining and bold face type. (And my aim in using them was to draw your attention to main ideas and important details.)

5.12 You would be wise to keep equally alert for the author's *verbal* signposts. Look out for words and phrases like:

firstly	for instance
on the other hand	furthermore
however	therefore

Such words are the author's way of telling you that he is about to list details, contradict a point, introduce a qualification, give examples, add to the strength of his main idea, state a conclusion, and so on. They act as *links* between one bit of his argument and the next, and should help you pick out the key ideas and significant details.

Can you see a 'verbal signpost' of this kind in the first sentence of the paragraph above, beginning 'You would be wise . . .'?

"equally" (This verbal signpost links frames 5.11 and 5.12 together by comparing the importance of the two kinds of signpost.)

5.13 *Diagrams and tables.* Many students miss a lot of main ideas and important details because they skip all the author's charts and graphs, tables and diagrams. Some think the diagrams are just there for decoration; others fear they may be too difficult to understand.

Diagrams and comprehension

Average test scores of three groups of students after a reading experiment in which

Groups A and B were given a text with illustrations while Group C was given the same text with the illustrations removed and only **Group A** was told to pay special attention to the illustrations.

The truth is, an author's illustrations should be read as carefully as his text. He will certainly not have used them simply to jolly up the page: space is too precious for that. A textbook author will only use tables and diagrams if he believes they will *teach better* than, and *instead of*, words.

So what is the *most important* reason for paying attention to the illustrations you come across in reading a book or article?

> They may help you to a better understanding of the main ideas and important details you've read in the text.   **A**
>
> They may make it unnecessary for you to read the text at all.   **B**
>
> They may carry main ideas and important details that are not mentioned in the text.   **C**

5.14   **A.** *Certainly this is one good reason for paying attention to tables and diagrams: they may clarify something in the text. However, it is not the* most *important reason. Please return to frame 5.13 and consider the alternatives again.*

B. *This is most unlikely. An author rarely gets enough space for all he wants to say; so he's not going to waste paper making every point both in words* and *in pictures. If you read only the pictures you'll miss some of his points, because some of them are made in words only. (Likewise, some points are made in pictures only.) Please return to frame 5.13 and re-consider the alternative answers.*

C. *Sometimes a picture saves a thousand words; sometimes it just saves a couple of dozen. But the author will rarely have space to repeat in print what he's already said very effectively with a diagram or table. Thus, the reader who skips illustrations may well be missing main ideas and important details that are not mentioned elsewhere in the text. Please go on to frame 5.15.*

5.15   So please don't regard an author's illustrations as mere decoration. But nor should you ignore them out of fear they may be difficult to read—they are rarely as complex as may appear at first sight.

Difficulties. This goes for most difficulties in reading—
whether with words or pictures. Try not to skate over
them in the hope they won't matter. If you leave a
difficulty unconquered you may:
1. lose confidence and begin to feel uneasy, and
2. be prevented from understanding later ideas.

So, if you come to an *important* paragraph or diagram
that you just can't make head nor tail of, what should
you do about it?
a. Forget about it and move on to more important
   material, or
b. Think extra hard about it, and even ask the advice of
   colleagues or tutors, or
c. Come back to it later, once you've mastered the rest of
   the text.

―――――――――――――――――――――――――――――――――――

b. (To forget about a difficulty, temporarily or
permanently, would probably run you straight into
further difficulties with the text.)

5.16 Now, *without looking back,* just check how much
attention you paid to the illustration I showed you on
frame 5.13. Try to answer these questions:
1. How many groups of students took part in the reading
   test?
2. How did the groups differ in the way they worked?
3. Which group scored best on the test right after the
   reading?
4. Which group scored worst?
5. Was the score of the second-best group closer to the
   best group's score or to that of the worst group?
6. Does the experiment suggest that all students pay
   attention to diagrams whether told to or not?
7. Did the group that scored best on the first test also
   score best on the retention test three days later?
8. Whose score had changed most: that of the best group
   or that of the other groups?

Well, that should be about enough to make my point. Please go back and *check* your answers (and decide the answer to any question that foxed you). Then when you are ready, go on to frame 5.17.

Let's hope you either (a) did quite well on that spot-check, or (b) resolved to keep a sharper eye on the illustrations another time.

Evaluate the Text

5.17 So *quality* of understanding depends on how well you can sort out the main ideas and important detail from the text you are reading. But it also depends on your ability to *evaluate* what you read.

By this I mean you should be a *sceptical* reader. Force the author to prove all his statements. Look for limitations, exceptions, contradictions, arguments against those he puts forward. Ask:
1. Are his facts correct?
2. Does he distinguish between facts and opinions?
3. Do his conclusions follow from the facts?
4. Would other conclusions follow equally well?
5. Do his conclusions agree with yours/your tutor's/other writers'?

To do all this you really have to get to grips with the book and relate all it says to your own experience. Look for your own *examples* and *applications* of what the author says.

What am *I* most concerned with in this book?
a. Having you remember my main ideas and important details so you can repeat them later in a test or exam.
b. Having you think critically about my suggestions and look for ways you might use them in your own work.

b. (I hope you are looking for applications for what I say, and are weighing up my remarks according to whether or not each one might be of use to you in your own studying.)

5.18 So far we have dealt with the factors affecting your quality of comprehension in reading. But understanding is not the only thing required from the effective reader.

Faster Reading

How long have you taken to read this programme so far? Whatever your answer, the odds are it's 50 per cent bigger than it need be. Most of us could read *half as fast again*—and still understand just as well.

The average adult reads at about 240 words per minute. But with a little training he should be able to raise this, without loss of comprehension, to about —— words per minute.

360 words per minute (that is, about 6 words a second)

Eyes and Brain

5.19 So why is it one person reads faster than another? And how can one increase one's speed? To answer these questions we need to consider what the eyes and brain are doing while we 'read'. To begin with, we all know that the eyes travel along a line of print from left to right (as yours are presumably doing now).

But how would you *describe* this movement from left to right?
a. a smooth, continuous sweep, or
b. a jerky, intermittent motion.

b. a jerky, intermittent motion. (Watch someone's eyes while he reads if you doubt this: you'll notice the split-second pauses.)

5.20 *Fixations.* The fact is that the brain can only recognise words when the eyes are still. So the eyes move along a line of print in a series of jerks, and after each jerk they stop briefly—they *fixate* on a piece of the text. (Your eyes may have made half a dozen such fixations in scanning the line above.)

At which points, then, is the brain 'reading' words? Is it . . .
a. at each fixation? or
b. between fixations? or
c. both?

a. at each fixation (lasting perhaps $\frac{1}{4}$ second)

5.21 *Recognition span.* Now at each fixation only about four *letters* will be in sharp focus. If you look at the word 'read' you see all the letters quite clearly. The words on either side ('word' and 'you') will be out of focus, and therefore less clear, but your brain will still recognise them.

The number of words you can recognise at one fixation is called your *recognition span.* If you couldn't see any words to either side of 'read', your recognition span would be one word—rather small. More likely, however, you'll be able to see two or three words at one glance. Some people, indeed, can take in a whole line at once, and thus read straight *down* a printed page.

Such people have an exceptionally large —— —— .

recognition span

5.22 So, when reading, your eyes move in a series of jerks interrupted by fixations. The number of fixations you need for a line of print will depend on how wide your recognition span is—how much of the line you can take in at once.

The bigger your recognition span, the (*more/fewer?*) fixations you'll need, and the (*faster/slower?*) you'll read.

___

fewer   *faster*

Poor Readers

5.23 The trouble with poor readers is that they have *small* recognition spans, so they are slowed down by the large number of fixations they have to make.

   The illustration below shows how a good reader and a poor reader might view the same couple of lines of print. Each vertical mark indicates a point of fixation (numbered to show the order in which it was made):

A. The unconscious mind seems to go on chewing away
    at a problem even though we have turned our attention
    to other matters.

B. The unconscious mind seems to go on chewing away
    at a problem even though we have turned our attention
    to other matters.

1. Which is the *poor* reader? A or B?
2. Altogether he makes about (*how many times?*) as many fixations as the good reader.
3. Partly this is due to his small —— —— .
4. N.B. But it is also partly due to the fact that he has several times looked *back* along the line to fixate on something he has already 'seen'. This has happened —— or —— times in each line.

___

1. *B* is the poor reader.
2. *twice* as many fixations.
3. small *recognition span*.
4. *two* or *three*.

5.24 *Regressions.* As you might guess from that last example, the poor reader has never really got beyond primary school reading ('read every word slowly and carefully') and he is still a 'word-by-worder'. In fact, he pays such individual attention to each word that he loses track of the overall meaning, and often forgets the beginning of the sentence before he gets to the end. So he can't keep his eyes moving (even slowly) from left to right: he has to move them back again to see what he's missed. These backward eye movements are called *regressions.*

As you noticed on the previous frame, the poor reader made at least two regressions per line, while the good reader made none at all.

Does a *good* reader *ever* make regressions?

─────────────────────────────────

Yes, but only when he is reading very difficult or badly written material.

5.25 *Vocalising.* There is one more fault common among poor readers (and another hangover from primary school days) —they *talk* themselves through a book. Of course, when we were first learning, we all used to read aloud. (Now we rarely do so except when entertaining other people or when consciously savouring the language of a text.) With practice, we have learned to read silently: but some people do it by talking to themselves. Even if they don't actually say the words aloud, they still go through the motions—moving their lips or making almost unnoticeable 'sub-vocal' movements in the throat.

Would you think this affects the *speed* of the reading, or the *quality*, or *both*, or *neither*?

Speed certainly suffers. It is difficult to read any text aloud at more than about 125 words a minute, while a fairly average 'silent' reader can manage more than 150 words a minute on a textbook and up to 600 words per minute on a novel.

Quality also suffers, because the 'vocalising' reader pores over one word at a time and so tends to lose sight of the sense of the sentence as a whole.

5.26 So we have picked out four faults associated with poor (slow and fuddled) reading:
1. Small recognition span
2. Many fixations
3. Frequent regressions
4. Vocalising

Now let's stop pretending that these faults belong exclusively to other people. We *all* suffer from one or more of them, even if only from time to time and in certain kinds of reading matter. We are all slower than we need or should be.

Think a moment about each of these four faults.
How would you set about *getting rid of it* if you found it occurring in your own reading?

See if you've anticipated any of the ideas I mention in the next few frames:

Five Ways to Improve Your Reading

5.27 To begin with, is it time you wore spectacles for reading? Unless you've had an eye test in the last two years, fix up to visit an *ophthalmologist*, or an *ophthalmic* optician (not just a seller of spectacles)—your college medical officer will help you find one. Many a student's reading problems have vanished once he's discovered (or admitted) his need for spectacles.

There are many obvious signs of eye defects: blurring and dancing of the print; tilting of the head and twisting of the face while reading; blinking and watering of the eyes, inflamed eyelids, and headaches after reading for quite a short while. But even the inability to concentrate *may* indicate a defect that could be corrected by wearing spectacles for reading.

If you had such a defect, what difference (*increase or decrease*) might a pair of spectacles make to:
1. The size of your recognition span?
2. The number of fixations you make?
3. The number of regressions you make?
4. The number of words you say aloud to yourself?
5. Your reading speed?
6. Your understanding?

---

1. *increase*
2. *decrease*
3. *decrease*
4. *decrease*
5. *increase*
6. *increase*

5.28 Secondly, *stop talking* to yourself. If you suspect you sometimes move your lips while reading, put your finger on them. This will both make you aware of the fault and prevent you from doing it.

But perhaps the best way of overcoming the habit is to read so —— that your lips just can't keep up with you!

---

fast (Although it may be rather circular advice, one way of learning to read faster is to start reading faster.)

5.29 Thirdly, then, *practise* reading faster. Stay alert, read with a sense of purpose, anticipate what you are about to read, and aim to get your eyes along that line of print as fast as possible. Don't regress to linger over something you've missed.

After all, which of these two approaches (if you were to spend an equal time on either) would be likely to give you the *better understanding* of a passage?

> Reading *each word* slowly and carefully, looking *back* to previous phrases to check points you weren't sure about.   **A**
>
> Reading the passage *twice* at something *close* to your top speed.   **B**

5.30 **A.** *This may sound like the safe and sure method, but I think you'd be disappointed with its results. Please glance back at frame 5.24 to remind yourself of the effects of word-by-word reading. Then read paragraph B below.*

B. *If you have any doubts at all about this 'speed' approach, do try it out when you next have the opportunity. You will find that even though you miss points on first reading (at just under your top speed) you will pick them up second time (in fact you may even manage a* third *'quick read' in the time it would have taken you to trudge laboriously from word to word). Go on to frame 5.31.*

5.31 Fourthly, read in *thought-units*. Stop reading word by word and look instead for the way words *group* themselves within each sentence. You should aim to read each group or 'thought-unit', at one glance. Indeed, your recognition span should take in a complete thought-unit.

A thought-unit may be a noun and its adjective, a verb and its adverb, or a short phrase, and so on. The thought-units in the last sentence of the previous paragraph are (to my mind): 'Indeed—your recognition span— should take in—a complete—thought-unit.' You don't have to read ten separate words in that sentence; you can swallow it in five gulps.

What are the major thought-units in the sentence you are reading right now?

Here is how I read the sentence:
'What are—the major—thought units—in the sentence— you are reading—right now?' (Is this more or less how you saw it?)

5.32 The good reader takes in about two words at one fixation in difficult material and three or more if the material is easy. By looking for thought-units he widens his recognition span and thus speeds up his reading.

Your recognition span depends also on one other very important factor (which you can definitely do something about). Read through the two sentences (1 and 2) below and decide:
a. Which of them can you read *more quickly* (with fewer fixations and regressions)?
b. Why is your recognition span *different* for each of the two sentences?

1. 'Her Hengest and Aesc his sunu gefuhton with Bryttas, on thaere stowe the is gecweden Creccanford, and thaer ofslogon feower thusenda wera.'
2. 'At this time Hengest and Aesc, his son, fought against the Britons at the place which is called Crayford and slew four thousand men.'

*Both sentences said exactly the same thing but unless you are
fluent in Anglo-Saxon, you:*
*a. Probably read (2) with fewer regressions and fixations.
(That is with larger recognition span, and thus more quickly.)
And:*
*b. Your recognition span for (1) was smaller because you were
unfamiliar with many of the words used.*

5.33 This brings us to the last, and very important, way of
improving your reading skills.

Fifthly, build up your *vocabulary*. The good reader knows
a lot of words. He therefore reads not only with greater
understanding, but also *faster*, because . . .
a. he can stop and consider the exact meaning of every
individual word? or
b. he can take in the meaning of several words at a
glance?

b. (The reader with a big vocabulary can take in the
meaning of several words at one glance and thus can
read faster.)

5.34 How big is *your* vocabulary? As a test, look at the words
in the list overleaf, which has been compiled (Kirkman,
1967) from the *Observer*, and the *Listener*, from editorials

in *New Scientist* and the *Engineer*, and from a novel, a
biography, and a work of social reportage. Ask yourself:

1. Could I *spell* each word correctly if I heard it read
   aloud?
2. Could I write each word in a *sentence* that would clearly
   show its meaning? (Use a dictionary if you need to
   check.)

complacent	reticence	inertia
emissary	dissemination	articulated
artefact	jeopardy	ubiquity
paradoxical	synthesis	tentative
misdemeanor	aberration	empirical
proliferate	omniscience	abstruse
unimpeachable	tenable	intuitively
autonomous	ostensibly	lucid
eradicate	atrophy	infallible
deducible	intractable	statutory
precursor	banality	intrepidly
insidious	collate	heretical
disparity	discern	immune
spectrum	anomaly	affluent
desultory	languid	adjacent
malignant	portent	dubious
infer	authentic	indigenous
scrutinise	inherent	disparagement
rationalist	propinquity	concomitants
unctuous	envisages	inexorably
efficacy	abject	precipitate (adj.)
altruism	indolence	transfiguring
categorically	cavilling (at)	sceptical
depravity	exponents (of)	benefactor

Count the number of words whose *meaning* you *do not*
know.

How did you score?

There were 72 words altogether. If you *missed:*

7 words or less	Quite likely you already read widely, quickly, and with clear understanding.
8 to 12	You probably have a reasonable vocabulary at this moment, but you should do all you can to keep it *growing*.
13 or more	You are almost certainly being held back by a weakness with words. You *must* give serious attention to increasing your vocabulary.

5.35 A wide vocabulary is essential, both for understanding other people's ideas (whether in speech or writing) and for expressing your own. Actually, of course, what we loosely speak of as *a* vocabulary is really *three* vocabularies (each of different size):

1. The words you use in speech
2. The words you use in writing.
3. The words you understand in reading (and listening).

Which of these three vocabularies is the *largest?* Which is *smallest?*

___

Probably your reading vocabulary is largest and your speaking vocabulary smallest. (Most of us can recognise words in print that we would hesitate to try out in our writing, let alone in speech.)

Vocabulary-building

5.36 But how does one build up one's word-power? Here are six useful steps towards a bigger vocabulary:

1. Read *widely* (not just in your own subjects).
2. Learn some of the common *Latin and Greek roots* on

which so many of our words are based. There is an
entertaining *programme* that will help you here (Davis,
1967).

3. Be on the *look-out* for new words, and *write them down*.

4. Get the *dictionary-habit:* Look up and note the meaning
of each new word as soon as possible after meeting it.

5. Use your new words in your writing (and speech) at
the first suitable opportunity.

6. Make your own *glossary* for technical words and phrases
that occur in your subjects.

So we've discussed five possible ways of improving your
reading—from having your eyes tested to expanding your
vocabulary. In which of the following *aspects* of reading
would you expect to see such improvements:

a. Speed with which you read?

b. Understanding of what you read?

c. Memory of what you have read?

==

a   *b*   *c*

(All these aspects of reading would be likely to improve
together.)

Practice Is Essential

5.37 If you want to improve your reading you must make a
conscious effort, and practice regularly. Set aside 15 to 20
minutes every day, perhaps just before you go to bed.
For the first few days stick to light reading, say *Readers'
Digest* (which does contain many *short* articles on a
variety of topics); then tackle some long articles in
newspapers like the *Guardian* or *Times*, or the *Sunday
Times* or *Observer* (or their colour magazines); then go on
to magazines like *New Statesman* or *Listener*; and then on
to more textbook-like material once you've built up your
stamina.

Tackle perhaps one or two articles every training session. Estimate the number of words in the article (fairly simple once you know the wordage of a full page or column), then see how quickly you can read it—time yourself to the nearest second.

Then try to *recall* what you've read—and check back through the article to see that you've picked out all the main ideas and important details. Don't worry if you miss a few at first, but keep trying to increase your speed *and* comprehension together. (This can all be a good deal easier, of course, if you can co-operate with a colleague: each can then time the other and ask him questions about what he has read.)

Keep a record of your speed on each article you read (preferably in *words per minute*). Draw a chart if you need a morale-booster! Within a couple of weeks you should begin to see a marked improvement.

What *other opportunities* (besides these nightly half-hours) would you have for practising faster and better reading?

Well I hope you'll be making a conscious effort to do all your study reading more rapidly. (After all, the purpose of the nightly sessions is to improve your reading skills for normal study; so why lose time before getting the benefits?)

Vary Your Pace

5.38 If you consciously strive, then, to increase your vocabulary and recognition span (and thereby make fewer fixations, and no regressions or sub-vocal noises) you will soon be able to read faster, with no loss of understanding.

But does this mean you will then romp through every bit of reading at exactly the same pace? No, it does not. Once you have learned to read faster you should be able to *vary* your speed according to what kind of material you are reading and what you are looking for. For instance:

1. With which reading *material* might you read more
     slowly?
   a. Novels, biography, and history, or
   b. Instruction manuals and textbooks.
2. For which reading *purpose* might you read more
     slowly?
   a. Looking for main ideas, or
   b. Looking for important details.

Probably: 1. b   2. b

5.39 So, whatever the nature and purpose of your reading, you will try to do it as quickly as possible. But since you cannot afford to sacrifice comprehension for speed, you will have to vary your pace to suit the occasion.

This does not mean, however, that you will need to fall back on word-by-word reading. If some material really does give you trouble, remember you may profit more from reading it several times at a little under your top speed than from ploughing slowly through it once. Yet even though you've 'taken in' each paragraph quite quickly, you may still appear to be 'slow' over the chapter as a whole. Why? Because you are not simply a recording machine. As a student—someone who is looking for *meanings*—you will often need to *pause for thought* between paragraphs, reflecting on the relationships between what you are reading now and your previous experience. All the same, with practice, your 'slow' reading speed may well turn out to be faster than what is now your maximum.

Bibliography
Davis, N. (1967)   *Vocabulary Improvement*
                          New York: McGraw-Hill
Kirkman, A. J. (1967)   'Command of Vocabulary Among University
                          Entrants' in *Education Research* IX2
Leedy, P. D. (1963)   *Read with Speed and Precision*
                          New York: McGraw-Hill

NB. Please *RECALL* this chapter (making some notes) and *REVIEW* it before you go on.

Then tackle the review questions that follow.

Review Questions

5.40 One basic way to improve reading is to make it active and purposeful by using the —— approach (Frame 2)

SQ3R

5.41 While reading a text you will be trying to do *three* things. What are they? (Frames 1–2)

Find the main ideas, pick out important details, evaluate the text.

5.42 Where would you normally expect to find the *main idea* of a paragraph? (Frames 3–7)

In the first or last sentence.

5.43 What are the two kinds of 'signpost' that can help the reader find the main ideas and important details? (Frames 11–12)

Visual (italics, underlining, etc.) and *verbal* (link words).

5.44 Why is it dangerous to skip the author's illustrations in reading? (Frames 13–16)

They may contain main ideas and important details that are not developed in the text.

5.45 State a question of the kind you might ask in *evaluating* a text. (Frames 17–18)

'*Is this true?*' is perhaps the most obvious question, but frame 5.17 lists several more, and you may have thought of yet others.

5.46 In the case of *poor* readers, which of the following tends to be *too large*, and which *too small*?
1. number of fixations
2. size of recognition span
3. number of regressions
4. amount of vocalising
(Frames 23–26)

1. *too large*   2. *too small*   3. *too large*   4. *too large*

5.47 List five possible ways of improving speed and comprehension in reading. (Frames 27–36)

Get eyes tested; stop 'talking'; practice reading faster; read in thought-units; increase vocabulary.

5.48 After regular practice in rapid reading, which of the following would you expect to be able to do?
1. Understand anything by reading at top speed.
2. Increase or decrease your reading speed according to circumstances.
3. Increase your average reading speed.
4. Keep up speed in future without further conscious effort.
5. Read everything at the same speed.
(Frames 37–39)

2 and 3

5.49 When you are ready, go on to Chapter 6, a very brief one, and make a conscious effort to read it more rapidly than you normally would.

6 How to learn from group discussion

(Study time: about 15 min)

With some topics of study you may be able to make quite satisfactory progress by reading and writing about them, listening to lectures, and carrying out any necessary practical work. This will be especially so, perhaps, in maths and science-based subjects. With many topics, however, especially in the arts and social sciences, you won't feel that you're getting your learning into perspective unless you have frequent opportunities to discuss the key issues with other students. You'll want to argue through the topics with your colleagues, exposing yourself to a variety of viewpoints and interpretations, and gaining both renewed enthusiasm and deepened understanding from the ebb and flow of discussion.

Opportunities for useful discussion may arise regularly and naturally in class work with your tutor. He may leave ten minutes or so at the end of a lecture for 'questions and discussion'. Or he may schedule sessions that are completely devoted to discussion of one kind or another. These may take many forms—from so-called 'simulation games' to group problem-solving exercises. Let's look at just a couple of basic forms which, if the tutor doesn't arrange enough of, the students can easily organise for themselves. One of these two forms I'll call 'a tutorial discussion' and the other 'a seminar'.

A Tutorial Discussion

This is normally led by a tutor who introduces the central topic or theme, arising perhaps out of a previous lecture or assignment, that the group is to consider. The group should be big enough to allow for a variety of knowledge and opinion, yet small enough to encourage and allow everyone to contribute—perhaps a dozen or so students at most. The atmosphere should be friendly and mutually supportive but all participants should have prepared in some way for the discussion. They must know enough about the topic to ensure that the discussion does not degenerate into either a lecture from the tutor or a public-bar swapping of unsupported prejudice.

There are several ways in which you can make best use of such a tutorial discussion:

1. Find out about the topic or theme in advance and read up on it.
2. Identify questions, issues, or contradictions that you would like to see aired in discussion.
3. Listen carefully to the opinions being expressed and the facts with which they are backed up; make occasional notes if this helps you concentrate.
4. Compare the facts with those known to you, and the opinions with your own. Challenge inaccurate or illogical statements—but politely!
5. If someone advances an opinion or argument that you don't understand, ask for it to be put another way.
6. Be prepared to ask questions or offer examples.
7. Put forward your own opinions for discussion. If your opinions are sound they will help others. If not, it's as well to get them out of your system before they become part of you.
8. If you know of an opinion or argument that would enrich or enliven the discussion, but which has not yet

been raised, put it forward even if it is not your own.

9. Help the group to keep the topic or theme in mind and avoid straying too far into side-issues that are of interest to a minority only.

10. Whenever you speak, keep to the point and be as succinct as possible. If your colleagues want you to elaborate, they'll ask you.

11. Don't be afraid of thoughtful silences.

12. Encourage colleagues who are having difficulty getting their ideas across.

13. If no one else is doing it, help the group from time to time by summing up progress to date (eg. 'We seem to agree on so-and-so, but disagree about such-and-such. Some say this while others say that. Is this a fair summary?') Such a summing up can be a valuable springboard to further discussion, and knowing that you may need to provide it will certainly help you keep alert.

14. Make a few notes afterwards to remind you of the main lines of the discussion and the state of your own opinions at the end of it.

A Seminar

In a typical seminar a student reads a paper he has prepared on a topic of common interest (speaking perhaps for ten minutes or more) and then defends it in discussion with his fellow-students. The role of the tutor is simply to help keep the discussion to the point, to ask the occasional clarifying question and perhaps, at the end, to sum up and throw in any opinions, references, or further evidence that have not been explored in discussion.

Clearly a seminar is of enormous benefit to the student presenting the paper. To do the job effectively he must select from a variety of data, prune and organise his ideas into a coherent thesis, and then present it logically and persuasively to his sympathetic but critical colleagues.

True, a certain amount of mild tension is inescapable for the presenter if he really cares about what he is doing but, in the informal and friendly atmosphere of a seminar, the effect is often to give him a lucidity and persuasiveness that he wouldn't normally lay claim to! If you do get a chance to prepare such a presentation, do make the most of it: you'll thus ensure that you know at least one topic inside out.

It is possible to get almost as much benefit out of criticising and commenting on a paper presented by someone else, provided you:

1. Read and think about the topic in advance.
2. Take an active part in the discussion along the lines suggested for a tutorial discussion.
3. Make some brief notes afterwards to sum up the speaker's main argument and the main points of discussion that followed.

Do-it-Yourself

If 'official' discussions don't occur as often as you and your colleagues would like, then do organise your own. Tutors do not have to be present in order for learning to take place. Students can undoubtedly learn a great deal from one another. Provided all participants in a discussion prepare adequately, and are able to admit that they do not know all there is to be known about the topic, there is no reason to fear that the blind will be led by the partially-sighted. Nor, provided they are willing to work for *one another's* understanding, need the situation be one where people think aloud but don't actually listen to one another.

Either the tutorial discussion or the seminar form can be followed, with a student appointed as chairman in place of a tutor. Appointing such a leader probably is a useful formality, especially if the group contains more than a dozen people. He can do a lot to ensure that everyone contributes, that 'super-stars' do not dominate the discussion, and that the atmosphere stays reasonably sweet! Actually, 6–8 students is probably about the right size for such a group. Much bigger and it might well tend to splinter into factions who just talk among themselves, anyway. Naturally, each member should be expected to take his turn at each of the tasks associated with the group—arranging the meeting, presenting a paper, being chairman, and so on. Hill's book (see below) gives very useful advice about the roles that need to be performed by group members and how to organise fruitful discussions. See also what I have to say in Chapter 8 about one special kind of student-run group— the revision syndidate.

Of course students also learn from each other in less formal situations. Useful discussions often spring up in corridors, in pubs, and on the bus going home. Even though you may not, in any strict sense, have prepared for such discussions, you should always be ready to participate as actively as possible *and* to make a *note* of any important points that emerge. (Remember the pocket notebook I advised you to carry always? page 68). And don't forget that students can learn from one another in groups of *two* as well as in larger gatherings. You will soon become aware of colleagues who have more grasp of a particular subject-area than you have and from whom you can occasionally seek discussion and advice. Similarly, you should be prepared to give some of your time to advising colleagues in those areas you are best at: not just out of natural kindness but also because the effort of sharing experience with someone else helps you get your own ideas sorted out.

Bibliography

Abercrombie, M. L. J.	*The Anatomy of Judgement*
(1960)	London: Hutchinson
Hill, W. F. (1969)	*Learning Thru Discussion*
	Beverly Hills, Calif.: Sage

6.1 How much do you RECALL after your first rapid reading of the chapter? For instance, what are the two main forms of discussion mentioned? How do they differ? Could you summarise the chapter's main points of advice in one sentence?
  1. Write notes on what you remember.
  2. Review the chapter (quickly), asking yourself the questions above. Then tackle the following review questions.

Review Questions

6.2 I believe this short chapter makes *three* main points about how to ensure you get maximum benefit from discussion groups. What are they? (Briefly skim the chapter again if necessary.)

The three points (which are pretty well spelled-out in the section about seminars) are:
1. Prepare 2. Actively participate 3. Make notes afterwards.

6.3 About which of these three main points are you given most 'important detail' in the chapter?

Eleven of the fourteen points listed in the section on tutorial discussions are important detail about how *to participate actively in discussion (No. 2). You will perhaps find it useful to return and re-read those points quite* slowly *(thinking about what they might mean for you) before you next take part in a discussion.*

6.4 One last question:
What is the minimum requirement for a useful discussion?
a. One tutor and one student, or
b. One tutor and two students, or.
c. Two students, or
d. More than two students.

---

c. Two students. (More students and a tutor will often be valuable but are not essential to useful discussion taking place.)

6.5 When you are ready, go on to Chapter 7 (and don't forget to apply what you learned in Chapter 5).

7 How to make notes

(Study time: about 45 min)

The Value of Notes

7.1 Poor or non-existent note-making is one of the common causes of failure for a student. Notes are a vitally important part of learning. Like the writing of essays, they give you practice in 'putting out' as well as 'taking in'.

Note-making helps in two ways: Firstly, it keeps you *active while* you are learning (thus aiding your concentration).

What is the *second* benefit you get (maybe weeks later) from having made notes?

You have a written record *from which you can* revise.

7.2 If you really want to get a grip on what you have heard or read it is far more valuable to put a few words on paper than to make do with a headful of hazy memories. The memories will soon drift away unless you pin them down in words, but you can keep your written record as a permanent reminder.

How to Store Notes

There are many ways of keeping your notes. Some will be more suited to your purpose than others. I describe below the practices of three different students.

Which of these methods would you consider most efficient?
a. Notes made on odd scraps of paper and the backs of envelopes; kept in a cardboard folder, or
b. Notes made on loose sheets of paper of uniform size; kept in a loose-leaf binder, or
c. Notes made and kept in a thick, hard-backed bound notebook.

Well I asked your opinion. I'm sure you scorned method a and made your choice between b and c. My own preference is for b—the loose-leaf binder. Although a bound notebook looks neater and easier to manage, it prevents you from arranging your notes in the most useful way.

7·3   Ideally you should be able to arrange your notebook so that *all* notes on a given topic are *together*—whether you got them from reading, lectures, or experiment, and whether you made them this term or last year. With a bound notebook, you are forced to store your notes in the order you wrote them, and the same topic may be dealt with in many different parts of the book. With a loose-leaf binder, on the other hand, you can re-order your pages, remove them, re-write them, and add new material at any point you wish.

So, suppose you've just made notes on Chapter 10 of a particular textbook. Where would you be most likely to store them?
a. In between the notes for Chapters 9 and 11, or
b. Directly after the last set of notes you took, or
c. Along with notes from other sources dealing with the same topic as Chapter 10.

---

c *I hope;* a *and* b *would be suitable places only if they happened to have notes on the* same topic *as Chapter 10.*

Writing the Notes

7·4 The main problem with notes is knowing what to put in and what to leave out. Working from books you get more time to make up your mind than you do in lectures but, ideally, the contents might be pretty much the same in either case.

Contents

Your notes should contain enough of the author's (or lecturer's) line of argument or discussion to bring it all clearly *back to mind* at a later date. Thus, your notebook must show:

a. The author's main ideas and any important supporting detail.

b. The logical plan of his argument (the hierarchy of ideas).

1. At *what step* of SQ3R do you begin to get some inkling of the *logical plan* of the author's argument (by examining headings, etc.)?

2. At *what step* do you confirm this impression and pick out the *main ideas* and *important detail* (by looking for topic sentences, etc.)?

---

1. *survey* (and possibly question)   2. *read*

7·5 So, you should pick out the key ideas and the way they are organised in the course of surveying, questioning, and reading.

You will then make your notes at the —— step of SQ3R, and check them against what you have read as part of the —— step.

7.6 Don't try to make notes until you've finished reading a section. Too many students read with one finger tracing along the lines of their book while the other hand diligently copies down great chunks from the text. All they end up with is a mini-textbook: when it comes to revision they might just as well re-read the original.

Remember that you are trying to recall only the *essentials* of the author's argument or discussion. Your aim should be to capture on two or three pages what he has said in twenty or thirty.

How should you word your notes?
a. Stick as closely as possible to the author's words, or
b. Use your own words as much as possible.

•

NB. Have you *surveyed* and asked *questions* about this chapter yet?

b. (*Mostly you should be using your own words—except where you need to record a specific quotation.*) *Your notes should be an expression of your understanding, not of your copying ability. Try not to look back at the author's words until you have sketched out some notes and are ready to review.*

Outline or Summary?

7.7 Broadly speaking, there are two ways of writing notes: as outlines or as summaries. While summaries are simply condensed versions of the original, still written in continuous prose, outlines (or skeleton notes) present the essential points in an almost diagrammatic fashion.

On the next two frames (frames 7.8 and 7.9) you'll see notes about Chapter 5 of this book made by two different students:

1. Which frame shows notes in *outline* form? 7.8 or 7.9?
2. Which notes more clearly show up the *logical relationships* within the chapter? Outline or summary?
3. Which notes would you find easier to *revise* from? Outline or summary?

When you have decided your answers, please go on to frame 7.10.

7.8 Notes from *Learn How To Study* (Ch. 5) by D. Rowntree
15.10.77

How to Read Better and Faster

I. Despite 'experience' few college students read as well as they might. (Too slow, can't concentrate, forget.)
II. For *better* reading (improved comprehension):
 A. Apply SQ3R to get sense of purpose.
 B. Look for topic sentence in each paragraph:
  1. Usually first or last sentence, and
  2. Contains the *main idea* of the paragraph.
 C. Look for important *details:*
  1. e.g. proof, example, or support for main idea.
  2. Usually at least one to each main idea.
 D. In hunt for main ideas and important details:
  1. Watch out for signposts:
   a. Visual (Layout and typestyles).
   b. Verbal (Clue words and phrases).
  2. Study all charts and tables.
  3. Don't skip difficulties.
 E. *Evaluate* the text:
  1. Be sceptical. (Expect author to prove.)
  2. Look for applications in your own experience.
III. Towards *faster* reading: (Most people could read half as fast again and still understand just as well.)
 A. During reading:
  1. Eyes jerk left to right in series of *fixations*.
  2. At each fixation, brain decodes group of words,
  3. Making up its *recognition span*.

B. *Poor* readers:
　　1. Have small recognition spans.
　　2. ∴ make many fixations.
　　3. Regress frequently. (Backward glances.)
　　4. Read aloud. (Or make sub-vocal noises.)
IV. Can improve reading. (Speed *and* understanding.)
　A. Five basic steps:
　　1. Check whether you need specs.
　　2. Stop saying words aloud.
　　3. Consciously try to read faster.
　　4. Read in thought-units. (2 or 3 words at a time.)
　　5. Build up vocabulary (reading, speaking, writing) by:
　　　a. Reading widely.
　　　b. Learning Greek and Latin roots.
　　　c. Noting new words.
　　　d. Using dictionary.
　　　e. Making glossaries.
　B. Practice (absolutely essential) by:
　　1. Nightly sessions (15–30 min.)
　　　a. Read articles of known length.
　　　b. Time yourself. (w.p.m.) (Progress chart?)
　　　c. Test your comprehension.
　　2. Reading *all* study material faster.
　C. Vary your reading pace:
　　1. Faster for 'story-like' material and main ideas.
　　2. Slower for complex argument and for important detail.

Compare these notes with those on frame 7.9. Then return to frame 7.7.

How to Read Better and Faster

Few college students have learned to read as well as they might: they read too slowly, they can't concentrate, and they don't remember what they have read. But they can usually improve by following some of these suggestions:

For improved comprehension, the reader should apply the SQ3R approach which will keep him *active* and *purposeful*. He should look for the *topic sentence* (usually the first or last) in each paragraph, for it will carry the paragraph's *main idea*. He will also need to look for the *important details* (examples, proofs, etc.) that go to support the main idea. (Usually there is at least one important detail to every main idea.) In his search for main ideas and important details he should be alert for visual and verbal *signposts* (clues to the author's meaning) and should pay proper attention to all charts and tables and diagrams. He should not skip over difficulties. The reader should also aim to *evaluate* the text by reading sceptically and looking for applications of what he reads.

Most people could increase their reading speed by 50 per cent without loss of understanding. During reading, the eyes move across the page from left to right in a series of quick jerks with stops (called *fixations*) in between: during the fixations, the brain registers a group of words (*recognition span*). Poor readers have small recognition spans and therefore make many fixations. They also take many backward glances (*regressions*) over what they have already seen, and they sometimes tend to mouth the words or say them aloud. All these faults help to slow them down.

A student can usually improve both his speed and his understanding in reading: he should check whether he needs reading-spectacles, prevent himself from saying words aloud, try consciously to read faster, read in thought-units, and *increase his vocabulary*. He can increase his vocabulary by wide reading, learning Greek and Latin word roots, taking note of new words, using the dictionary, and making glossaries in his own subjects. Practice is essential and can be applied both to normal study reading and to regular nightly sessions. In these nightly sessions ($\frac{1}{4}$-hour minimum) the student should read articles of known length, time himself, and calculate his speed in words per minute, and then test his understanding of the content. Once he has increased his ability to read at speed, he will be able to *vary* his reading speed to suit his material and his purpose: faster perhaps with novels, biography, and history, and when looking for main ideas; more slowly with instructional manuals, textbooks, and when looking for important details.

Compare these notes with those on frame 7.8. Then return to frame 7.7.

1. *Frame 7.8 shows an outline (7.9 a summary).*
2. *The outline shows up the relationships more clearly.*
3. *The outline is probably easier to revise from.*

7.10 *Writing an outline.* Where possible, try to outline rather than summarise your reading and your lectures. Here's how to begin outlining a text:

Get a skeleton for your outline from the author's *headings* (if he has used them). Expand each heading into a *sentence* containing the main idea of the section or sub-section it belongs to.

Especially when headings are few, you will also need to look at the topic sentence of each paragraph in the section. It probably carries a main idea that you will need to put in your notes to help develop the argument.

If you want to include *important details*, enclose them in *brackets*.

Look back to frame 7.8 (and, if necessary, to Chapter 5) to see how our student handled this in his outline. *What else* has he done—in order to show up the *logical plan* of the argument?

As you'll have noticed, the student did turn each of my headings into a sentence containing a main idea; he got further items for his outline from the topic sentences of my paragraphs; he put important details in brackets. In addition—*to show up the structure of the argument*—*he set his note-items in from the margin and added* letters *and* numbers.

7.11 So, having picked out the main ideas (of sections, sub-sections, and paragraphs), you *indent* them from the margin, according to their relative importance. Main items start *at* the margin. Second-order items are indented by, say, half an inch. Third-order items go in by another half inch, and so on.

Don't indent too little, or the relationships won't be clear. Don't indent too much, or you won't have room for your notes.

In the outline notes on frame 7.8 there are four main items, ten second-order items, twenty-five third-order items, and (*how many?*) fourth-order items.

ten *fourth-order items*. (IID1a, IVA5d, etc.)

7.12 As you've noticed, that last outline used not only indentation but *also* letters and numbers. To show how your notes hang together you need a system of lettering and numbering that will emphasise the relationships. For example:

Main items	Roman numerals (large)	I, II, III, IV
2nd order	Capital letters	A, B, C, D
3rd order	Arabic numerals	1, 2, 3, 4
4th order	Lower-case letters	a, b, c, d
5th order	Roman numerals (small)	i, ii, iii, iv

And if you need extra orders you can always start putting brackets around Arabic numerals (1), or around lower-case letters (a).

On the next frame you will see an outline for Chapter 4 of this book. (In fact, it is the outline from which I *wrote* the chapter; but it is also the sort of outline you should be able to make from reading it.)
However, I've left a few of the letters and numbers out. Will you please *complete the job.*

7.13 (*Did* your *notes for the chapter look anything like this?*)

How to Write Essays

I. Writing essays can help a student in 3 ways:
    A. Forces him to organise his thinking
    B. Shows up his strengths and weaknesses.
    C. Prepares him for exam situation.
II. Make sure you *understand* the essay task:
    A. What is the precise subject?
    B. What kind of treatment called for?
III. How to *collect* suitable material:
    A. Think out questions to guide your research.
    B. Begin thinking right away in order to:
       1. Make yourself alert for relevant ideas.
       2. Give unconscious mind a chance.
    C. Keep a notebook for essay ideas.
    D. Investigate all possible sources of information:
       1. Books, articles, etc. suggested by tutor.
       2. ,,   ,,   ,,   ,,   by those books (or library staff).
    E. Note the source of all materials you collect.

IV. Spend time *planning* the essay:
  A. Select the most useful of your material:
    1. Throw out the trivial, irrelevant, or obscure.
    2. But keep enough detail to support your argument.
  — Write a logical outline.
    — This ensures that you:
      — Sort out the main ideas and important details.
      — Miss nothing vital.
      — Write fluently.
      — Get extra marks in exams.
    — One basic outline framework is:
      — Introduction—comment on subject and your treatment.
      — Main body—your argument in 3 or 4 main ideas.
      — Conclusion—summary and final comment.
  — Write the final paragraph.
— Write the *first draft* of your essay:
  A. Write simply and directly.
  B. Let layout reveal structure of argument.
  C. Use pictures if they can save words.
  D. Clearly distinguish your ideas from other people's.
  E. Write a bibliography.
VI. *Re-write* the essay after a few days:
  A. Check for and eliminate weaknesses of content or treatment.
  B. Make sure final draft is neat, and clearly-written.

  C. Keep a copy.
When you have filled in the missing numbers and letters (12 of them altogether) turn to frame 7.14.

The numbers and letters you should have filled in are (in order):
B. 1. a. b. c. d. 2. a. b.
C. C. V.

7.14 So here is how to write good outline notes from a book:
  1. Expand the author's *headings* and re-state *topic sentences* so as to get items that express the main ideas of sections and paragraphs.
  2. Write any important detail in brackets.
  3. Lay out your items using *indentation* to show which comes under which.
  4. Letter and number the items to make this relationship even clearer.

Now make a brief outline based on the first few headings (and some extra words and phrases) from Chapter 3.(You'll need to glance back at the chapter.) Just *expand* the phrases below, *indent* them as you see fit, and *add* your numbers and letters.

SQ3R: Survey   **Surveying a Book**
Title page   Preface   Table of Contents
Leaf through the book   **Surveying a Chapter**
First and last paragraphs   Summaries   Headings
(Topics dealt with. How they relate) Question

When you have finished your outline, check with frame 7.15.

Does your outline look anything like the one below?

SQ3R (Survey, question, read, recall, review) is a useful approach to studying a text, and consists of the following steps:

I. *Survey* first to get a general view of what you will then study in detail:

   A. Survey the book as a whole.

      1. Glance at the title page.

      2. Read the preface.

      3. Examine the table of contents.

      4. Leaf through the book.

   B. Survey each chapter in more detail before you study it.

      1. Read the first and last paragraphs.

      2. Read any summaries.

      3. Examine the headings to discover:

         a. What topics are dealt with.

         b. How they relate to one another.

II. Look for *questions* that will give purpose to your reading.

7.15   Now the outlining method obviously gives you a very useful set of notes from which it is easy to revise—you can see the gist of the matter at a glance. I hope you'll find plenty of use for it in the future (if it isn't already your normal method).

Writing a summary. But what about the summary? Are there some subjects or topics in which it would be preferable to write your notes in straight prose, in continuous paragraphs?

Can you think of any kinds of reading you do for which such *summary* notes might be *preferable*?

Of course your answer will depend on your subject, and the kinds of reading you have to do. Possibly in some parts of language learning, or mathematics, a summary will be preferable. Again, with literature or some aspects of history, you may find that what you need to refresh your memory is a synopsis, a summary, or even an appreciation or critique—written in continuous prose.

7.16 But if you do decide to write a prose summary, keep it short, and make it as easy to revise from as possible. This brings us to another important aspect of making notes—how to set them down on the page.

The Mechanics of Notemaking

And the first question here is: How good is your *handwriting*? Will your notes be clear and readable to you, perhaps a year or more after you wrote them? (A recent survey at one university showed that more than 60 per cent of the students had difficulty in reading their own notes.)

Obviously your notes will be no use to you if you can't —— them. One way of making them more legible than even the best handwriting could, would be to —— them.

---

read   type (The student who can type up his notes is at a considerable advantage: provided he *re-thinks* them while he types.)

7.17 But even if you decide to use a typewriter you can't, of course, take it into lectures (or into examinations), so you'll still have to make sure your handwriting is reasonably legible.

Abbreviations. In lectures, particularly, your handwriting may suffer because you are trying to get too many ideas down too fast. One way of keeping up your speed without scribbling is to work out a set of abbreviations.

For instance, you should have short ways of writing special terms that are common in your particular subject. In Psychology, for example, you might usefully have contractions for words like: 'experiment, behaviour, conditioning, memory, correlation, gestalt, psychology,' and so on.

And for common phrases that are needed in practically every subject, you'll probably know most of the fairly standard abbreviations below:

e.g.	i.e.	c.f.	N.B.	$=$	$\neq$	$<$	$>$	$\therefore$	$\because$

Can you match them against these phrases?:
1. greater than
2. less than
3. because
4. therefore
5. equals, is the same as
6. compare, remember in this context
7. does not equal, is different from
8. note well, important
9. that is
10. for example

1. *greater than* ($>$)
2. *less than* ($<$)
3. *because* ($\because$)
4. *therefore* ($\therefore$)
5. *equals, is the same as* ($=$)
6. *compare, remember in this context* (c.f.)
7. *does not equal, is different from* ($\neq$)
8. *note well, important* (N.B.)
9. *that is* (i.e.)
10. *for example* (e.g.)

7.18 There are only two rules with abbreviations:
First: Make up your system and stick to it. (Don't chop and change.)
Second: Don't use your abbreviations in material other people will have to read.

Layout. Use every trick of layout you can to make your notes *look memorable*—as an arrangement on the page. The more logical and/or dramatic they look on the page, the more easily you will be able to picture them in your mind's eye. And this will help in examinations.

Which kind of notes are automatically laid out in a logical, almost 'pictorial' fashion?
a. Summaries, or
b. Outlines.

b. *outlines*

7.19 To make summary notes as effective as an outline, you'll have to go to a bit more trouble with spacing and layout. (Do *not* try to make them look like paragraphs in a book.)

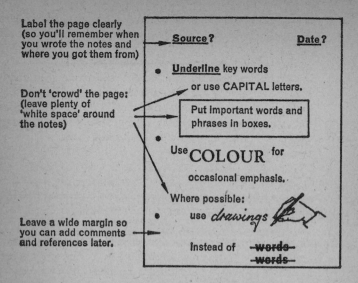

Label the page clearly (so you'll remember when you wrote the notes and where you got them from)

Don't 'crowd' the page: (leave plenty of 'white space' around the notes)

Leave a wide margin so you can add comments and references later.

Source?   Date?

- <u>Underline</u> key words or use CAPITAL letters.

Put important words and phrases in boxes.

- Use COLOUR for occasional emphasis.

Where possible: use *drawings*

- Instead of ~~words words~~

With your page of notes laid out in this fashion, you should be able to close your eyes and bring the notes back to mind as a *picture*. (Try it now with the page shown above.)

How will this *help* you?

You should find it easier to remember the wording of your notes if you can picture the layout. (Well-spaced notes are always easier to recall than a cramped and crowded page.)

Making Notes in Lectures

7.20   Despite the practical difficulties of the lecture situation, your *aim* should be to produce easily-read *outlines* of the kind you would make from your reading.

Use SQ3R

The best approach to a lecture is to use the SQ3R technique, as far as you can. *Surveying* a lecture in advance is something you can't easily do, but you should be alert for any remarks from the lecturer that indicate the ground he is to cover.

Questioning, however, may not be so difficult. Presumably you know what was said last time, you may have done some reading, and you perhaps have some expectations about what is to come. Approach the lecture in a critical, questioning state of mind, and keep framing questions (even if you don't need to ask them) throughout.

In lectures, of course, you don't *read:* instead you —— .

listen

7.21 And the *listen* step involves you in a very complex task. Simultaneously, you must hear, analyse, select, and record. Not only must you pick out the lecturer's *main ideas* as he speaks, and grasp the *overall structure* of his argument, but also, and *at the same time,* you must string together a set of readable *notes* that will bring it all back to mind.

In what ways can a skilful lecturer help to make this task simpler for you?

He can write his main headings on the chalk-board; he can preview at the beginning of each section and summarise at the end; he can draw your attention to the most vital points. (You may have thought of yet other ways.)

7.22 Admittedly, not all lecturers are equally helpful in this, and your note-making tactics will have to be flexible enough to cope with quite a variety of individual lecturing styles. Even so, you will sometimes find it extremely difficult to organise your notes as you are writing them, or even to be sure of what the main points are supposed to be.

Some students deal with this by taking copious notes and hoping to see some pattern emerge from them by the time the lecture ends. Others struggle to grasp the lecturer's line of argument, taking very few notes even if it means missing out some of the main points.

Do you tend to take a great many notes in lectures, or very few? Why?

Possibly your practice will vary from one lecture to another. (It might pay you to try and account for the differences.)

7.23 On the whole, it is perhaps better to err on the side of too *few* notes rather than too many, *provided:*

1. This better enables you to grasp the essentials of the lecturer's argument.

2. You are prepared to write up a full set of notes soon after the lecture is over.

But this brings us to the next, *vitally important*, step in applying SQ3R to the lecture situation:

Having done your best to *survey*, *question*, and *listen* to the lecture, you must now try to —— what was said.

recall

7.24 Never be content with your notes as they stand at the end of a lecture. By comparison with reading-notes they are almost certain to be *incomplete* and somewhat *disorganised*. Go away and re-think them. With your notes in front of you, try to *re-construct* the lecture in your memory.

This first attempt at recall is something many students shy away from, yet it can dramatically halt the process of forgetting. (*Without* an attempt at recall, most students forget 75 per cent of what they have heard in a lecture within one week—and in less than three weeks they have forgotten 98 per cent of it.)

How soon after the lecture should you first force yourself to recall what you have heard?
a. Immediately after, or
b. One week later, or
c. More than one week later.

---

a. *Immediately after.* (*Even then you may remember only 50 per cent of what was said.*)

7.25 While the lecture is still fresh in your mind you can think it through again, correcting your misunderstandings, adding detail to your notes, and giving them more shape. Discipline yourself to do this *within a few hours* of every lecture and you'll reap huge benefits; leave it too long and you may find your lecture notes simply don't make sense.

In the course of trying to *recall*, you may often wish you could take the final step of the SQ3R method:
That is, you wish you could ——— what was actually said.

---

review

7.26 Unfortunately, you can't review (or re-hear) the actual words spoken (unless the lecture was tape-recorded). But what you can do, if you sense a worrying gap in your notes, is go and ask the lecturer about it. Normally, he will be happy to review any point that has eluded you.

Who else can you check with, besides the lecturer?

You can check with colleagues who attended the lecture with you. Did they get points, or see some theme or structure of ideas, that you missed?

7.27 If you and some of your fellow-students are agreed on the need to improve note-making, you might sit down and check each other's notes after each lecture (and maybe after a piece of reading you've all done also).

A Check-list

Perhaps your group could agree on a checklist of faults that your notes should avoid. Here is one such list:

1. *General Format*
   a. Notebook too small/big
   b. Pages too crowded/spread out
   c. Handwriting illegible
   d. Topics mixed together
2. *Structure of Notes*
   a. Poor labelling at top
   b. Not in outline form (too much solid prose)
   c. Insufficient use of headings, numbers, indents, emphasis
   d. Hard to see organisation and relationships of ideas.
3. *Content and Phrasing*
   a. Missed some of main ideas
   b. Too much detail
   c. Too wordy
   d. Wording unclear
   e. Too much in author's words, not own
   f. Missed, or misdrew, important graphs, tables, etc.

Once a checklist was agreed, each set of notes could be assessed by each student in the group, and all should learn from the ensuing discussion.

NB. Don't forget to *RECALL* and *REVIEW* this chapter before going further.

Then tackle the review questions.

Review Questions

7.28 What are the *two* main benefits to be had from writing notes? (Frames 1–2)

Note-making keeps you actively concentrating, and provides a written record from which you can revise.

7.29 What is the advantage of using a *loose-leaf* binder for your notes? (Frame 3)

You are not tied down by the order in which you wrote your notes: you can re-arrange them under topics as you wish, re-write individual pages, and add to them at any point.

7.30 At what stage of SQ3R is it best to make notes? (Frames 5–6)
a. At the *read* step, or
b. Between *read* and *recall*, or
c. At the *recall* step.

c. *At the* recall *step. (At the read step you would be too close to the author's words, and there is no step between read and recall.)*

7.31 If you haven't done so already, make an *outline* of the chapter (7) you have just read. (Frames 7–15)

How does your outline compare with this one?
I. The *value* of notes is that they:
   A. Keep you active and concentrating.
   B. Provide a written record for revision.
II. Store notes in a loose-leaf binder (for flexibility).
III. *Writing* the notes:
   A. Contents should include:
      1. Author's main ideas and important detail.
      2. Logical plan of his argument. (Essentials only)

B. Make notes at *recall* step.

C. Use your own words.

D. Use *outline* form (rather than summary) where possible:

    1. Expand headings and re-state topic sentences.

    2. Put important detail in brackets.

    3. Use indentation, and

    4. ... letters and numbers } to show up relationships.

E. *Mechanics:*

    1. Write clearly or type.

    2. Work out set of abbreviations.

    3. Use logical/dramatic layout on page:

        a. New page for each set of notes—label clearly.

        b. Plenty of 'white space', and wide margins.

        c. Colour, diagrams, emphasise key points, etc.

IV. In *lectures:*

A. Try to use SQ3R

B. Write few notes rather than many, if:

    1. This enables you to follow the lecturer's argument.

    2. You write up fuller notes soon after lecture.

C. Check and revise your notes within a few hours of the lecture:

    1. Re-construct the lecture in your mind (recall).

    2. Correct your notes, add detail, give them shape.

D. Review lecture by discussion with:

    1. Tutors.

    2. Colleagues (Compare notes against group checklist?).

7.32 Do you believe a page of summary notes should be densely-packed with the vital information or that it should carry fewer ideas, more widely-spaced? Why?
(Frames 18–20)

*Well-spaced notes are usually preferable, even though they use
up more paper. The less you put on one page, the more easily
you can picture it and bring it back to mind.*

7.33 In applying SQ3R to a lecture, what would you do at the
recall step? *When* would you do it? (Frames 24–25)

*As soon as possible after the lecture, you would try to
re-construct the lecture in your mind, correct your notes, add
detail, and put them into a more organised shape.*

7.34 How might you 'review' the lecture to check the
accuracy of your recall? (Frames 26–27)

*You could check with colleagues who also heard the lecture, or
even with the lecturer himself.*

7.35 Now we come to the final chapter—How to Deal with
Examinations. Like Chapters 4 and 6, this chapter also is
in continuous (umprogrammed) prose: but it has far
fewer headings or 'visual signposts' to help the reader.
Thus (while still 'easy meat' compared with many
textbooks) it gives you a rather more demanding test of
your ability to sort out main ideas and the way they are
organised.

So, when you are ready to go on:
1. Study Chapter 8, using all five steps of the SQ3R
   approach. (You will probably need to recall at least
   twice *before* you reach the end of the chapter.)
2. Write a well-organised set of *outline* notes. (These
   should run to about two sides of A4 or quarto paper.)

8 How to deal with examinations

(Study time: about 40 min)

Whatever we may think of them, examinations are part of our way of life. A student hardly needs to be told this. He realises that examinations are going to help determine his future. Regular (termly or yearly) examinations still decide whether, or under what conditions, he is allowed to continue his course; a final examination will decide whether or not he gets the qualification awarded to those who have successfully completed the course.

Since not only personal self-esteem but also career prospects may dwindle drastically if the final qualification is not obtained, there is little wonder that many students approach examinations with some anxiety. Unfortunately, this can get out of hand. While a certain amount of mild tension is unavoidable (and may indeed be psychologically valuable) some students take refuge in 'examination nerves' as an escape from the unconscious guilt they feel at having wasted the time that leads up to the examination: by 'going to pieces' they hope to attract sympathy instead of blame. (No one who has worked through the programme so far could possibly fall into this category!)

Basically, the situation is this: Examinations are put together and marked in such a way that the student who has satisfied the entry requirements for his particular course can perform reasonably well in the exam— *provided* he has applied his intelligence to the course and has prepared properly. If he fails to do himself justice in the examination it will probably be because of faults either in his *preparation*, or in his examination *techniques*.

So what can the student do to ensure he is properly prepared? How can he perform to the best of his ability on the day of the examination? These are the questions we'll try to answer in this final chapter.

Preparing for Examinations

The surest way to examination success is to conscientiously apply effective study techniques over a period of time. If you even approximately follow the advice we've worked out in this book (timetabling your study, SQ3R, systematic note-making, etc.) your chances will be enormously improved. You will remember more, have a better understanding, and be able to organise your ideas quickly and effectively. Such skills are rewarded in examinations as they are in other areas of human activity.

Of course, the key role in preparing for tests and examinations is played by *revision*. Literally, this means 'to see again'. Few of us can grasp an idea in all its possible aspects and applications simply from one exposure to it. We need to 'see it again', often many times and preferably from many different angles, before it really becomes part of our understanding.

When should you start revising for an examination? The answer is *now*. To get results, revision must be a regular part of your study routine, right from the beginning of your course. All the time, as you meet new ideas, you should be looking back over the ideas you have already met, testing and refreshing your memory about them, and 'seeing them again' in the light of your more recent experience.

There are two very good reasons for doing regular revision right from the start. For one thing, you simply wouldn't have the time (or peace of mind) to revise everything in your course if you left it all to the last minute. Secondly, and more important, early revisions will make later material *easier to learn* since you will already have a firm understanding of what precedes it:

the more you have learned, the easier it is to learn more.

As the examination draws near, of course, you will need to be quite systematic about your revision. For the final five or six weeks you should work out a revision *timetable*. Make a list of the topics that have to be revised, and decide what order they should be tackled in. Space out the revision for each topic and make a note of what you intend to revise during each day of your revision timetable. To keep up interest it is usually better to revise a *variety* of topics each day rather than devote yourself to one topic exclusively. Don't forget to leave plenty of time for rest and recreation, *especially* in the last few days before the examination.

So revision must start early in your course as a regular part of the routine of study. As examinations approach it must be timetabled very seriously, so that you don't find you've left everything till the last week. All right, we know *when* to revise: the next question is *how?*

One very valuable way to revise is to join up with a couple of fellow-students who are doing the same course as you, and meet together two or three times a week to revise topics as a *syndicate*. Clearly, you have to make sure you can all get on together, and it does demand a certain maturity of outlook and self-discipline to ensure that such revision sessions remain purposeful and do not degenerate into trivial chit-chat. But the benefits of working as a member of a syndicate rather than on your own are great enough to make the effort worthwhile.

For one thing, it helps you be much more objective about the course. Working by yourself you can be so attracted by one area of the syllabus that you completely overlook some other equally vital areas. Within a group, however, other people's preferences are likely to differ from yours, and you can help make each other aware of the syllabus as a whole, and thus the possible coverage of the examination paper.

Also, on account of this difference of interests, each

member of the syndicate is likely to find himself
'teaching' the others whenever his special topics come
under discussion. And, as all teachers know, the best
way to learn something yourself is to teach it to
somebody else.

Psychologically also, it is valuable to work as a
member of a revision syndicate, rather than in solitary
confinement. The human contact can help you keep a
sense of proportion about the impending event, and
thereby lessens the anxiety that might otherwise build up.

In order to revise for an examination it should be
obvious that you must find out all you can about that
examination. Get hold of a copy of the syllabus: What
topics are prescribed? Look at past examination papers:
What sort of questions are asked? Are questions on some
topics compulsory? How long do you get to answer each
question?

The reason I suggest finding out all you can about the
syllabus and the examination is that, during your revision,
you should *practise doing what the examination will require
you to do*.

For instance, the examination will aim to measure what
you can *recall* from your studying. So, in revising, you
should put the emphasis on recall rather than on
re-reading. As I've mentioned before, the fact that you
can recognise ideas when you read them again is no
guarantee that you'd recall them in an examination.
Therefore, when you come to read your notes again and
perhaps check the textbooks, you should only do so
after having tried to recall the main ideas they contain.

Furthermore, it is unlikely that the examination paper
will require you to display your facts and ideas in the
same form they were in when you first came across them.
In the examination you will be called upon to *re-combine*
your ideas and use them in *new ways*. Try to re-organise
your knowledge, form new associations of ideas, and
look at things from many points of view. Apart from

being a more appropriate training for the examination-job, this approach is also more interesting than if you were drearily to retrace your original learning path.

Revising as a member of a syndicate is a very good way of learning to look at a topic in a new light. In a group of three or four students there are usually four or five opinions, and a topic does seem to take on a new significance once it has been the subject of a heated debate.

It is also helpful in re-organising your learning if you revise all your material on a particular topic at once. Take all your notes (whether from textbooks, tapes, films, lectures or seminars) along with your essays and old examination answers, and work on them all together. Viewed again in this way, you may see associations of ideas that were not evident before, and you may clear up earlier misunderstandings.

Similarly, it can be illuminating to revise two or three *related* topics at the same time. Although you first studied them separately you may now find many common strands linking the topics together. Thus you get to see each topic in a new light and you have an extra set of associations to help jog your memory.

In trying to get new viewpoints, *force* yourself to view differently. In working through your old notes and essays, be critical. This shouldn't be too difficult. After all, you are now older (whether by weeks, months, or years) than you were when you wrote them. Do they now seem at all unclear, ignorant, muddled, misguided, cock-sure, one-sided, embarrassing? Try to uncover their weaknesses. Hunt out your omissions and faults of emphasis. Assault your notes and essays with the newer ideas and more mature viewpoints you will have acquired since you first wrote them. Use them as an opportunity to test out your newer understandings.

Then re-write your notes ruthlessly. Write summaries and condensed outlines that contain the essential ideas of all your original notes and essays on a topic but which are much shorter and which you've up-dated in the light of more recent experience.

So it is advisable to emphasise *recall* and *re-organisation* of knowledge in your revision, because these will be the general activities rquired of you in the examination. But it is wise to practise also the more specific skill required of you: that is, the *answering of examination questions*.

For most examinations the question papers from previous years are available. Get a set of papers and analyse the questions that have been asked over the last few years. Collect questions together according to topic. Then try to answer them.

Don't just browse through the papers telling yourself 'Yes, I could manage numbers 1, 4, and 7, but I'd be in trouble with 2, 3 and 6'. You can't really be sure of how you'd do until you actually practise answering such questions.

One of the most useful ways of giving yourself practice is simply to write answers in *outline* form. Weigh up the question, decide what it is asking for, then jot down the main ideas and important detail that you would want to bring into your answer. Then write down the key steps of your argument as a skeleton outline, just as you would before writing a normal essay.

A similar approach can be used in a revision syndicate. Each member can show or speak his outline to the rest of the group and have his argument discussed. Clearly it can be valuable for all members to answer the same question, for comparison of the different answers may be instructive for everyone. Another variation is for the group to take half a dozen questions on a common topic, revise around that topic, and allocate a question at random for each member of the group to answer. And, of course, members can also make up their own questions for colleagues to answer.

Since planning is the most crucial step in answering a question, you will be pretty safe in spending most of your practice time in writing plans for answers. (Especially since you can plan two or three answers in the time it would take you to plan and write out the complete answer for just one question.)

However, at least now and again, you would be wise to write out complete *model answers*. Time yourself, though. Work out how long you would be allowed in the examination room and then both plan and write your essay within that time. Some students even find it helpful to spend one morning a week for the last two or three weeks actually putting themselves through a mock examination. That is, they sit down with an unfamiliar paper and, under examination conditions, spend three hours or whatever is allowed in coming up with the best answers they can manage. If you have any doubts about your ability to concentrate and work flat out for the period of the examination, this is an excellent way of breaking yourself in—so at least you won't expire from shock on the day. Again, these dummy runs can be even more useful if done within your revision syndicate and followed up by comparison of answers and discussion.

Keep all your practice answers, whether outline notes or full essays. They will be particularly valuable for last-minute revision of vital topics.

One warning. In the course of your revision you may find yourself predicting that certain questions are 'bound' to come up in your exam. Have bets with yourself by all means, but don't pin too much reliance on being right. Certainly don't neglect other areas of the syllabus: don't over-specialise. Students have been trying to out-guess examiners for years and they never succeed: the examiners have always been at it longer than any student.

To sum up, successful revision needs to be started early: it demands that you find out all you can about the examination and that you practise doing the things you will have to do in the examination room (that is, putting-out ideas, rather than taking-in); and it is often most useful if done as a member of a revision syndicate.

All too soon perhaps, your revision timetable has been eaten away and you reach the last day before the examination. Students spend this day in a variety of ways, according to temperament. Some believe in switching off all conscious thought of the exam and doing no work at all. For others it is so difficult to keep their minds off the exam that they find it less of a strain simply to continue normal revision. If you are one who must keep at it, make absolutely sure it *is* revision you are doing, and not new learning. Trying to learn new things at this stage would only block out things you've learned previously.

One thing you can profitably do the evening before the examination is to make sure you have all the items of equipment you'll need next day: a watch, a couple of pens (with ink), pencils, ruler, mathematical instruments, and whatever else is likely to be useful for the paper you'll be sitting.

If you do spend the last day revising, make sure you break off at least two hours before bed-time (or you'll be carrying on relentlessly in your sleep). Read something entertaining, watch television, or chat with any of your friends who are not obsessed by examinations. Go to bed early and get a good night's sleep. Remember that next morning a fresh alert mind will be far more useful to you than a few extra facts packed in behind a sickening headache.

The Day of the Examination

Some wit has pointed out that most students sit each examination three times: on the bus going to the examination hall, again when they get there, and a third time on the bus going home. And unfortunately they only get credit for one of these performances.

If you can, avoid doing a 'preview' on the way to the examination. Especially avoid talking about the prospects with other candidates: you'll only get depressed and dispirited at the thought of all the topics you should have paid attention to and haven't. Keep to yourself, and remain confident that you've done everything humanly possible (because if you haven't it's now too late to worry). If you must think about the forthcoming paper, let your thoughts be specific: concentrate on just one possible question and organise an outline answer in your mind.

So, at last, the moment arrives. You are mildly tense, keyed-up to respond to the challenge, but you are certainly not in fear and trembling. You are *prepared*.

Once you have the examination paper in your hand, read it *right through* very carefully. Too many students hunt frantically for the first question that looks vaguely familiar, let out a gasp of relief, and plunge straight into an answer without so much as a glance at the other questions or the instructions to candidates.

Spend at least the first five minutes of your time just reading through and getting the 'feel' of the paper. Look first at the instructions to candidates. How long have you got for the paper? How many questions do you have to answer? Do any of them carry more marks than others? Are any of them compulsory? Is the paper divided into two or more sections, with so many questions to be answered from each? Does each answer have to be started on a new sheet of paper? And so on.

You'll probably know most of these answers from your practice with previous papers, but it pays to check, for the rules may have been changed. Every examination brings its rueful crop of students who've spoiled their chances by answering four questions instead of three (or vice versa), or who didn't realise they had to answer *all* the questions in Section A, or who thought they had three hours, (not two) for the paper, and so on.

Then pay individual attention to each and every question. Make sure that you know what each question is asking for (even if you can't provide the answer), and also what it is *not* asking for. Be objective, and don't misread the questions. Don't try (as many students do) to twist them into the questions you *wish* had been asked.

You must also be sure of *precisely* what the question requires you to *do*. Look for the key *verb* that tells you what kind of answer to give. Here is a list of the ones most commonly used in examination questions:

Analyse	Illustrate
Assess	Interpret
Comment	Justify
Compare	List
Contrast	Outline
Criticise	Prove
Define	Reconcile
Describe	Relate
Discuss	Review
Enumerate	State
Evaluate	Summarise
Explain	Trace

Needless to say, if you 'describe' when you are asked to 'analyse' or if you 'define' instead of 'enumerating' you have failed to answer the question. And you'll get no credit if you simply 'write around' the subject. If you are in any doubt about the differences in meaning among these twenty-odd verbs, you'd be wise to go to a good dictionary and compile your own glossary of 'examinese'.

After you have considered every question on the paper, and perhaps put a pencil mark against those that seem 'possibles' you should be ready to make your final choice. Be very wise in this. Avoid if you can the 'easy' question that everybody can answer: the examiner will soon tire of wading through the hack responses and he won't thank you for adding to them. Look for questions that will allow you to show your own personal flair. But, at the same time, don't get out of your depth by taking on a question that's too tough for you: there are no marks for bravery.

The next step (yes, you may not have written a word yet), is to *budget your time*. How long can you spend on each question? The best plan is to allocate your time according to the number of marks allowed for each question. If all carry equal marks then you divide your time up equally. So you have perhaps four questions to answer in three hours. How long per question? Not three-quarters of an hour, for you'll have used up five or ten minutes by the time you come to start planning your first answer, and you should allow yourself another ten or fifteen minutes spare at the end for a final check-up on all answers. So, you may decide you have forty minutes or less to spend on each question. Look at the clock and write down the *actual times* by which you expect to have finished each question.

You are now ready to plan out your answers. Before you begin writing you should have a *skeleton outline* of the kind we have discussed before: more than ever, in the time-limited examination situation, you need this as a firm guide to your writing. Furthermore, even if you decide not to submit the outline on your answer paper, the examiner will be impressed with its results, for your answer will be a logical, well-organised argument rather than a rag-bag of jumbled out-pourings. (Besides, students who have run out of time in an examination have often got almost as many marks for submitting a clear outline as they would have been awarded for a complete essay.)

With each question, then, jot down the main ideas and important details that occur to you. Do a bit of free association and just let the ideas come to mind as they will. Not all will be equally useful, but make a note of them regardless. Then sort them out, and write an outline of your argument in the usual way. At least a quarter of your total 'answer time' should be spent planning and outlining.

Some students would recommend that you outline *every* answer before writing out any one of them in full. There are three benefits to be had from this approach: Firstly, you can more easily treat your answers as a set, and avoid the possibility of repeating yourself from one to another. Secondly, you are giving your unconscious mind a chance to work for you: having planned out all the answers, your unconscious is likely to carry on the train of thought even while you are writing the first answers, and so may come up with fresh associations that will help you in writing the later ones. Thirdly, once the preliminary planning is complete, you have the comfort of knowing exactly what ground you've got to cover in the remainder of the time, and all you have left to do is expand on your outlines. It takes nerve to spend perhaps the first hour in writing the complete set of detailed outlines, but the results can be very rewarding.

Once you start writing your answers, success or failure depends on your *sense of priorities*. Begin by answering your best question (or the compulsory question if there is one). Keep your mind on one question at a time but be prepared to jot down any ideas that may suddenly occur to you for use in other answers.

Watch the clock and stick firmly to the time-limits you set yourself. If you run out of time on a particular answer (or if you get bogged-down on it), *stop writing*. Leave a big space on your answer sheet in case you can come back to finish off later, but get right on with the next question. In the peculiar arithmetic of examinations, $\frac{1}{2} + \frac{1}{2}$ is usually greater than 1, and two half-answered questions will normally earn you more marks than one complete answer. Many students fail because they spend too long on their 'best' questions.

In your writing, concentrate on saying what is most worth saying: if you are running short of time, get the main ideas down and don't worry too much about the detail. Be concise: very often 50 per cent could be cut from a student's answer without losing him marks.

The style of your written answers should be the same as that of other essays you write—simple, direct, and to the point. Pay attention to spelling and grammar: be particularly careful not to mis-spell words that appear on the question paper. But, above all, *write legibly*. Your answer sheets have to be read and marked by human beings, not machines; and if they find difficulty reading your words they are likely to be less sympathetic towards your ideas.

Don't rush away from the examination room the moment you've written your last full stop. Save yourself a few minutes at the end to give all your answers a final check: you should search for slips of the pen (a vital 'not' left out of a sentence), for miscalculations (in numerical examples), for clumsy expressions, for faulty spelling or grammar, and for illegible phrases that can be re-written. Such a final check is never a waste of time: it is simply a professional way to finish off the job, and many a student picks up five to ten per cent of his final mark in this last round-up. Besides, it is better to have a last-minute inspiration while checking through your paper than while going home on the bus.

But, when it really is all over, don't hang around for those depressing post-mortems with other students. They rarely make you joyful about the answers you have written, and too often they leave you brooding about all the things you've left unsaid. This can be very unsettling if you have another examination looming up; so it's best to get right away, enjoy some rest and recreation, and then resume training for your next bout with the examiner.

Learning from Examinations

In conclusion, it's worth remembering that most examinations are *not* end-of-course examinations, and it is possible to *learn* from your performance in them. The typical student pays very little attention to his answer paper if it is returned to him (other than to moan about the mark and check whether the examiner has added any amusing comments); but very often it could teach him a lot about how to prepare for the next exam.

If you have your paper returned, analyse each answer against the original question, and consider the examiner's comments and grading. If possible, compare your answer with those of other students, and ask your tutors for comment. Where did you lose credit? Did you misinterpret the question? Did you leave out some important ideas or some vital supporting detail? Was your answer badly-planned or illogical? Did you misunderstand some vital part of the course? Or did your memory let you down? How would you write the answer if this question were to come up again? How can you avoid having the same trouble with another question in a later examination? By analysing your mistakes in this way you can uncover faults in your study technique and remedy them before it is too late.

8.1 Now:

1. *Recall* the final section, and the chapter as a whole.
2. Finish off your *outline notes.*
3. *Review* the whole chapter to check and tidy up your outline.

Then, before you compare your outline with that drawn up by another reader, work through the following review questions. (They may remind you of something your outline has overlooked.)

Review Questions

8.2 Suppose you have to sit an examination one year from now: about when should you *begin* to revise for it? (Page 137)

Begin now.

8.3 Which of the following activities should you stress most in your revision: reading; recalling; reviewing? Why? (Page 139)

The emphasis should be on recalling, *because this is what you will be required to do in the examination itself.*

8.4 The examination will also require you to re-combine your ideas and use them in new ways. Describe at least two ways of preparing yourself for this. (Page 140)

You can discuss topics with other students; you can revise all your notes from all sources (on a given topic) at once; you can revise two related topics at the same time you; can be ruthless in criticising and re-writing your old notes.

8.5 What is the third thing—a specific skill—that a written examination will require of you? How can you prepare yourself? (Page 141)

The writing of essays. You can prepare yourself by working with past papers: plan outline answers, write complete model answers, sit mock exams.

8.6 What are all the preliminary jobs you must do between getting the examination paper in your hand and beginning to write out an answer to your first question? (Page 144)

Read through the paper (checking instructions, weighing-up questions, and deciding which ones to answer); budget your time; write outline plans for at least one of your answers.

8.7 If you were pressed for time, would you prefer to hand in one answer completely written out in detail, or two answers outlined in skeleton form? Why? (Page 147)

Two well-planned outlines would be likely to get you more marks than one answer written out in full.

8.8 What would you do if you finished writing your last answer and found you still had ten minutes left before the end of the examination? (Page 148)

Presumably you would use the time to check through all your answers and add the finishing touches that might well add appreciably to your overall mark.

8.9 And now:
CHECK your outline against the following one, which was written by one of the students who helped me test this programme by reading it through before publication. Did you pick out the same 'hierarchy of ideas' as he did? Did you include more or less detail? Have you noted anything vital that he has missed, or vice versa?

How to Deal with Examinations (Good preparation +
exam technique).

I. Examination success demands *preparation:*

  A. Apply effective study techniques over period of time.

  B. Revise systematically:

    1. Start *now;* because

      a. Never enough time later.

      b. Future work will come more easily.

    2. Make a *timetable* for revision.

      a. Space out revision for each topic.

      b. Tackle variety of topics each day.

      c. Allow plenty rest and recreation.

    3. Form a revision *syndicate* (3 colleagues, 3 times a
week).

      a. Fosters objectivity

      b. Learn by teaching others.

      c. Keeps you sane.

    4. Practice doing what the exam *requires* of you:

      a. Emphasis on recall (not recognition).

      b. Re-organise your ideas by:

        i. Discussing with others.

        ii. Revising *all* notes on a topic at once.

        iii. Revising related topics together.

        iv. Criticising own notes.

        v. Re-writing notes.

      c. Tackle old examination papers:

        i. Write outline plans for answers.

        ii. Write complete model answers.

        iii. Sit mock exams.

        iv. Don't try to out-guess examiner.

  C. On the *day before* the exam:

    1. Do not learn *new* things.

    2. Revise normally or relax completely.

    3. Gather exam equipment.

    4. Go to bed early.

II. *Technique* on the day of the examination:
  A. Don't discuss prospects with other students.
  B. Read right through exam paper (5 min):
    1. What instructions to candidates?
    2. Decide what each question is asking for (key verbs)
    3. Choose your best questions.
  C. *Budget* your time:
    1. Allocate total time according to marks per question.
    2. Leave 10–15 minutes at end for checking.
    3. Note expected finishing time for each question.
  D. Plan your answers:
    1. Jot down main ideas and important details.
    2. Form them into a skeleton outline.
    3. Outline *all* answers before writing any up? $\frac{1}{4}+$ of all 'answer time')
  E. Keep a sense of *priorities:*
    1. Answer best question first.
    2. Stick to your time-budget ($\frac{1}{2} + \frac{1}{2} > 1$!)
    3. Concentrate on main issues.
  F. Write:
    1. Simply, directly, and to the point.
    2. Grammatically, and without mis-spelling.
    3. Legibly.
  G. When finished writing:
    1. Check through all answers (till time is up).
    2. Don't stay for post-mortem discussions.
III. *Learn* from examinations by:
  A. Checking examiner's marks and comments against questions.
  B. Comparing your answers with other students'.
  C. Discussing your performance with tutor.
  D. Remedying any faults revealed in study techniques.

Finally:

Please remember that my purpose in this book has not been to teach you how to study but to persuade you to teach yourself. At the very least, I hope I have convinced you that study is a job with its own professional work skills; and I believe we have worked out a way of talking about this job that will enable you to examine future study problems objectively and discuss them fruitfully with tutors and colleagues. All that's left now is for me to wish you GOOD LUCK in all your studies and examinations.

Bibliography

(In case you might wish to give yourself a 'refresher course' from time to time!)

Armstrong, W. H. (1956) *Study is Hard Work* New York: Harper

Barker, L. A. (1971) *Listening Behaviour* Englewood Cliffs, N.J.: Prentice Hall

Beveridge, W. M. (1965) *The Art of Study* London: Oxford

Bird, C. & D. M. (1945) *Learning More by Effective Study* New York: Appleton-Century-Crofts

Bjernum, V. (1971) *Study Technique* London: Harrap

Bono, E. de (1971) *The Use of Lateral Thinking* London: Penguin

Buzan, T. (1971) *Speed Reading* London: Sphere

Corfield, T. (1967) *How to Be a Student* London: Workers' Educational Association

Courtney, J. V. (1970) *Study for Success* London: Tutertext

Diack, H. (1967) *101 Aids to Exam Success* London: Dickins

Diack, H. (1967) *Study—The Easy Way* London: Corgi

Emmett, E. R. (1965)	*Learning to Think* London: Longman
**Hill W. F. (1969)	*Learning Thru Discussion* Beverly Hills, Calif.: Sage
Hills, P. J. (1973)	*Study to Succeed* London: Pan
**James, D. E. (1967)	*A Student's Guide to Efficient Study* London: Pergamon
Jones, E. (1974)	*Effective Writing* London: Ward Lock
Laing A. (1963)	*The Art of Study* University of Leeds
**Leedy, P. D. (1963)	*Read With Speed and Precision* New York: McGraw-Hill
**Leeuw, E. & M. de (1966)	*Read Better, Read Faster* London: Penguin
Lindgren, H. C. (1969)	*The Psychology of College Success* London: Wiley
Maddox, H. (1963)	*How to Study* London: Pan
**Morgan, C. T. & Deese, J. (1957)	*How to Study* New York: McGraw-Hill
Orchard, N. E. (1953)	*Study Successfully: 18 Keys to Better Work* New York: McGraw-Hill
Parsons, C. J. (1973)	*Theses & Project Work* London: Allen & Unwin
**Pitkin, W. B. (1962)	*The Art of Rapid Reading* New York: Grosset & Dunlap
Reid, J. F. (1973)	*A Guide to Effective Study* University of Edinburgh
Robinson, F. P. (1946)	*Effective Study* New York: Harper
Styler, W. E. (1963)	*How to Study* London: Worker's Educational Association

**Woodley, C. H. (1959)   *How to Study* Sydney: Angus
                             & Robertson
And for a glimpse at the other side of the coin:
Beard, R. (1970)   *Teaching & Learning in Higher
                             Education:* London: Penguin
Layton, David (ed) (1968) *University Teaching in
                             Transition*
                             Edinburgh: Oliver & Boyd
(** particularly recommended)

Index

The entries in this index refer mainly to frame numbers. However, the entries for Chapters 4, 6, and 8 where there is continuous prose without frame numbers, are identified by page numbers.